Honoré Daumier
1808-1879

The Armand Hammer Daumier Collection
Incorporating a Collection from George Longstreet

The Armand Hammer Foundation makes possible exchanges of art, sponsors medical research and promotes international understanding for the progress of people everywhere.

This exhibition is made possible by The Armand Hammer Foundation

Cover:
Scène de Comédie
Two Actors ca. 1870-73
Oil on panel
24.7 x 31.8 cm

Contents

Dedication

To my wife Frances, who shares my interest and appreciation of the arts and whose name is linked with mine on the Frances and Armand Hammer Wing of the Los Angeles County Museum of Art.

Armand Hammer

Foreword

I have always enjoyed Daumier the artist. I was naturally attracted to his work. There is something about his energy and productivity that I admire. The lines in his drawings and lithographs seem to be alive with intensity. While my appreciation of his work grew, I learned more about Daumier the man, about his personal courage, his compassion, and his love of humanity. Daumier the man and artist became an irresistible attraction for my collecting.

The first opportunity to acquire an important work by Daumier came at the Goldsmith sale in 1970 when I purchased the watercolor *The Pleading Lawyer* (cat. no. 186). In 1976, I was able to acquire a collection of Daumier lithographs asssembled over a fifty-one year period by George Longstreet. This collection of more than four thousand different examples is said to be the largest Daumier collection in private hands. It is a great satisfaction for me to know that this collection serves as a comprehensive resource for studying the work of Honoré Daumier.

Since that time, I have been fortunate to expand my collection by adding six important oils including *The Lawyers* (cat. no. 184), *Don Quixote and Sancho Panza* (cat. no. 185), *The Reading Lesson* (cat. no. 237), *Two Actors* (cat. no. 239), *The Picture Connoisseurs* (cat. no. 240) and *Head of a Bell-ringer* (cat. no. 241); more than a dozen drawings and watercolors; thirty-eight sculptures; and a rare lithographic stone on which is etched one of Daumier's original drawings.

We tend to judge art according to our own times. Even though these works were created more than one hundred years ago, there is something extraordinarily relevant about them today. Daumier has been quoted as having said "one must be of one's own time." But because Daumier had the genius of perception and the ability to record his impressions in art, we the people of today can see — as if firsthand — the attitudes of Paris and the history of France reproduced before us in this exhibition.

My joy in assembling this collection is exceeded only by sharing it. I plan to travel the collection worldwide to promote international understanding and world peace. The first showing of this Daumier exhibition outside the United States was in Mexico City in 1980. Other cities scheduled to receive the exhibition in the early 1980s are London, Oslo, Edinburgh, New Orleans and Atlanta. Eventually, the traveling exhibition will join the thousands of other works in my collection in a special Daumier study center which I have made possible at the Los Angeles County Museum of Art. There, scholars and students will be able to do research on one of the world's greatest artists. I am continually rewarded by the knowledge that so many individuals are able to observe the genius of Daumier through my collection.

Armand Hammer

Preface

Honoré-Victorin Daumier died on February 11, 1879. His legacy is the greatest number of visual images created by any artist from antiquity to the end of the nineteenth century. This includes about 4,000 lithographs drawn directly on the stone, about 1,000 wood engravings, more than half of which were drawn on the block, over 800 watercolors and drawings, about 300 oil paintings, and a small number of extant sculptures. Since his lithographs were printed in large editions, often from 1,000 to 3,000 each, and his wood engravings in multiple, though smaller editions, Daumier was responsible for more than 5,000,000 original works of art! This does not mean that Daumier offers no challenge to the collector. Most of the lithographs for newspapers and periodicals were discarded and lost, some were disapproved by the censor and never published, and there were always rare impressions before publication. These include the one to three extremely rare proofs of the lithographs on heavy ivory or colored paper made before the addition of lettering; the two or three proofs on thin ivory paper with the title, legend and identification of printer, one or two of which were for the censor; the fifty proofs on heavy white paper of many of the lithographs printed by Aubert; and the proofs of wood engravings on thin India paper on which Daumier often wrote *bon à tirer* or initialed his approval. With this vast quantity of material, common and rare, comprehensive exhibitions of Daumier's work have perforce been selective.

The association of Armand Hammer and Honoré Daumier is so logical that it seems to have been inevitable. Dr. Hammer has a deep conviction that works of art can bring enjoyment on many levels to people from the simplest to the most sophisticated if they are only given the opportunity to see them. Consequently, he has made his collection of paintings and drawings available to regional museums across this country as well as to exhibition centers in Europe, South America, Mexico and Japan, where it has always drawn a broad cross section of the population. Daumier created his lithographs as Baudelaire wrote, for the entire populace of Paris, "the bourgeois, the businessman, the urchin and the housewife," who could delight in his political wit and find their own identity or that of their acquaintances in his vignettes of human nature. But his appeal extended likewise to artists like Delacroix, Corot and Daubigny, the photographer Nadar, and writers like Michelet, Balzac and Baudelaire. Consequently, when the Daumier collection of George Longstreet became available, Dr. Hammer did not hesitate to acquire it with the intention of augmenting it and eventually presenting it to the Los Angeles County Museum of Art so that it would be permanently accessible to students, scholars, collectors and the public.

George Longstreet bought his first Daumier lithograph from a bookstall along the Seine for a nickel at the age of sixteen while visiting his aunt in Paris. Before the summer was over he had acquired forty more at the same price. For the first twenty years his aim was to obtain an example of every known Daumier print; for the next thirty his goal was to refine the collection by acquiring fine impressions and bound volumes.

When Dr. Hammer acquired the collection in 1976, it was the largest in private hands in the country, consisting of more than 4,000 lithographs and woodcuts, excluding duplicates but including the complete *La Caricature* bound in ten volumes, twenty-three bound semesters of *Charivari*, along with bound volumes of other periodicals for which Daumier worked. Since rarities in the collection are in the exhibition and will be noted in the catalogue entries, I shall mention here only that five of the lithographs are not in Delteil's *catalogue raisonné* of Daumier's prints, and at least one is not in the Bibliothèque Nationale in Paris, the most complete collection of Daumier prints in the world.

Dr. Hammer, conscious of the close interrelation of all of Daumier's work, has added six oil paintings, watercolors, more than a dozen drawings, thirty-eight bronzes, a lithographic stone, and has expanded the print collection with over two hundred lithographs, including sixteen proofs before the letter, of which one was censored, a group of wood engravings and the only poster Daumier ever designed.

The guest curator for the Los Angeles Daumier exhibition was one of America's most eminent scholars and connoisseurs of prints, Elizabeth Mongan. Beginning in 1939, Miss Mongan was Curator of the Lessing Rosenwald Collection at Jenkintown, Pennsylvania, and as that collection became part of the National Gallery in Washington, she served also as Curator of Prints there from 1941 to 1963. She has organized exhibitions, written and lectured extensively on French graphic art of the nineteenth century; her *catalogue raisonné* of the graphic work of Paul Gauguin is in progress. As guest curator, Miss Mongan selected the pieces for exhibition and compiled the catalogue. Through the generosity of M. Jean Adhémar, for many years Chief Curator of the *Cabinet des Estampes* at the Bibliothèque Nationale in Paris, Miss Mongan is able to publish here the names and biographical sketches of twenty-one heretofore unidentified members of the Chamber of Deputies portrayed by Daumier. Miss Mongan's sister Agnes, who wrote the introductory essay, was Curator of Drawings at the Fogg Museum from 1947 to 1975 and shares her sister's distinction as a specialist in nineteenth century French graphic art.

In planning a Daumier exhibition that is largely graphic, it is difficult to decide whether to place emphasis on the quality of drawing, composition and impression, and the rarity of state that will delight the connoisseur and collector, or to explore in depth and breadth Daumier's panorama of Parisian life that will satisfy the curiosity of the public and of the political and cultural historian, but which requires a much larger number of prints. Miss Mongan explains her choice and organization of the material in the following words: "This exhibition affords an unusual opportunity for the public to see, at one time, the scope of Daumier's graphic genius. Examples were chosen not necessarily for their rarity, but to illustrate the diversity of themes and the development of the artist from youth to maturity. The exhibition becomes inevitably a splendid panorama of nineteenth century France. This history of costume, manners, fads and politics are all to be found in these inimitable pictures."

Kenneth Donahue
Director Emeritus
Los Angeles County Museum of Art

Acknowledgments

An exhibition from the Armand Hammer Daumier Collection was originally organized by the Los Angeles County Museum of Art in 1979 to commemorate the centennial of Daumier's death. It was subsequently shown in Washington, D.C. at the Corcoran Gallery of Art and in Mexico City at the Cloister of Sor Juana. The first European museums to host the Daumier Collection are the Royal Academy of Arts, London and the National Gallery, Oslo. It is with great pleasure that The Armand Hammer Foundation shares this exhibition with institutions in the United States and abroad and we are grateful for the cooperation of all those involved in presenting Daumier's phenomenal achievements to the public.

Many individuals are responsible for organizing this exhibition and catalogue. In addition to the curators mentioned in Kenneth Donahue's remarks, there are several individuals who deserve special mention: Mr. Donahue has been a valuable consultant and has graciously prepared catalogue entries for new acquisitions; Jeanne d'Andrea, curator of exhibitions and publications, Los Angeles County Museum of Art has been an indispensable liaison between The Armand Hammer Foundation and exhibitors of the Daumier Collection; Martha Wade Kaufman, former curator of The Armand Hammer Collection and director of art of the The Armand Hammer Foundation who was involved in the development of this exhibition and earlier editions of the catalogue; Warren Kennaugh designed and Sheri Hirst supervised production of this catalogue.

We would also like to thank George Longstreet for his years of devotion to Daumier and his continued support of the Foundation's efforts to make this collection of Daumier's work one of the best in the world.

Dennis A. Gould
Director
The Armand Hammer Foundation

Quinton Hallett
Assistant Director
The Armand Hammer Foundation

Introduction

In his essay "Daumier Caricaturist," published in *Century Magazine* in January 1890, Henry James ventured the opinion that "many people would tell us that journalism is the greatest invention of our Age...it touches the fine arts, touches manners and morals...journalism is the criticism of the moment *at* the moment, and caricature is that criticism at once simplified and intensified by a plastic form...." The famous American writer was stirred to write the essay, it seems, in order to explain to himself the extraordinary delight he had experienced in looking through piles of Daumier lithographs which he came upon in one of the Parisian bookshops on the Left Bank of the Seine.

Turning and re-turning those illustrated pages increased the writer's pleasure, his puzzlement, and his desire to explain both. He makes no mention of the medium of lithography, an invention of the opening years of that very century.

When Henry James wrote, less than a dozen years after Daumier's death, little had been written about the artist. The intervening years have seen the publication of a long list of learned monographs, written by French, German, English and American critics. Outside as well as inside France, the number of his devotees has grown enormously, yet the known details of his life remain few. To a degree that seems unique, his life was his art. In the more than four thousand lithographs which we have from his hand can be found his philosophy, his political opinions, his interests, his inclinations, and above all his never failing humanity.

That six of his eight great-grandparents were natives of the rocky heights of the Maritime Alps tells us something of his inheritance. That, in Paris, men as gifted and as different as Corot and Baudelaire were among his good friends tells us a good deal. That the boy from Marseilles, who had little formal schooling, became, as the years passed, intimately familiar with the works of Rabelais, Racine, Molière and Cervantes is both startling and sobering.

In the past thirty years much has been learned about his few masterful, memorable paintings and his incomparable drawings. Both were little known when he died a hundred years ago. The problems of his sculpture are still being elucidated. His real monument, one cherished by a wide international public, remains that formed by his prints. A century after his death, they delight us as they delighted the newspaper readers of his time. They make clear that man and his foibles have not changed. We can recognize situations, implications and subtleties, relish Daumier's art, and be warned by signs whose message does not change.

The Paris that the young glazier's son from Marseilles came to know was one which changed greatly in aspect as well as in politics during his lifetime. Revolutions, uprisings, riots and wars were familiar happenings. The bourgeoisie became powerful; the Romantic Era flourished and passed; Baron Haussmann changed the appearance of the city; omnibus routes came into use and quickly grew in number; the railroad train became commonplace. Yet the inhabitants of that city, the rascals, the swindlers, and pretentious politicians and the pompous judges were not unique to that time nor that place, nor were the poor, the unfortunate, the decrepit and the abandoned.

As Daumier draws them there is sometimes an element of the sinister, but it is subtly counterbalanced by the comic. As the artist grows in experience and in command of his medium, as his line becomes simpler but more powerful, his subject matter shifts from the politics of the day to the theater, to the courtroom, then to the larger theme of *La Comédie Humaine*. Throughout his life he remains a patriotic Frenchman who seeks the best for his nation. He remains also a profound humanist.

Paul Valéry, the distinguished French writer of the first half of the twentieth century, in his essay on Daumier, comments on the fact that the French graphic artist is often compared to Michelangelo and Rembrandt, a comparison Valéry finds justified. In that triumvirate, the French writer feels that Michelangelo is the theologian of mankind, Rembrandt the philosopher, and Daumier the moralist. In the moralist's role, although he can entertain us as we observe the daily scene, more importantly, through his unfailing tolerance and deep human understanding, he can instruct us.

Agnes Mongan

Chronology

1789	20 June	The Oath in the *Jeu de Paume*
	14 July	Seizure of the Bastille
	August	Declaration of Human Rights
1791	20 June	Flight of the Royal Family of Varennes
1792	10 August	Capture of the Tuileries. Fall of King Louis XVI. Reign of Terror — Robespierre
1794	27 July	(9 Thermidor)
1799	9 November	(18 Brumaire) The Consulate
1804	18 May	Napoleon I, Emperor
1808	26 February	Birth of Daumier
1814	8 April	Abdication of Napoleon. Departure for Elba. 1st Restoration
1815	1 March	Departure of Napoleon for the Golfe Juan
	19 March	Louis XVIII leaves Paris. Napoleon's 100 days
	18 June	Waterloo. Napoleon defeated. Return of Louis XVIII. White Terror. Descazes. Daumier in Paris
1824		Death of Louis XVIII. Charles X on the throne. Return of the Ultras Ministry of Marignac then Polignac
1830		Publication of the laws of Charles X suspending the liberty of the press. July Revolution
1831		Uprisings in Lyon and Paris. Ministry of Casimir Périer
1832		Riots in Paris. Lawsuits against the press. (*Le National, La Tribune, La Caricature*). Daumier, Philipon and Aubert condemned to six months in prison effective 31st August
1833		Ministry of de Broglie with Soult, Thiers, D'Argout, Rigny and Guizot
1834		Publication of *Le Ventre Législatif*. Riots in Lyon. Riots in Paris. The massacre in Rue Transnonain
1835		Lawsuit against the Accused of April — called the Monstrous Trial. New laws suppressing liberty of the press
1848	24 February	Abdication of King Louis-Philippe
	20 December	Louis-Napoleon elected President of the Second Republic
1849	July	New laws restricting the press
1850	May	Law against universal suffrage
1851		Repression of Republican resistance
	2 December	Louis-Napoleon's *coup d'état*
1852		The Constitution of 1852
	9 November	Louis-Napoleon declared Emperor
1859		The Italian War
1870		Declaration of War
	19 July	Defeat of Sedan
	2 September	Capitulation. Abdication of Napoleon III
	September	German armies besiege Paris. Declaration of war on Prussia
1871		Armistice. The Commune. Thiers
1875		Marshal MacMahon. President of the Third Republic. Passage of constitutional laws
1879	11 February	Death of Daumier

Explanatory Notes

The abbreviation "Del." refers to the first great catalogue of Daumier's lithographs compiled by Loys Delteil, published in ten volumes 1925-1926. In each catalogue entry, the state and publication date of the lithographs are given. The state of the lithograph exhibited here is not necessarily the one actually published. The bibliography at the end of this catalogue is a brief selection from the enormous number of books, articles and exhibition catalogues that are now in print on the artist.

The legends printed at the bottom of the prints were in the early years composed by Philipon or others in the *Charivari* offices. It was only in the late great prints of the 60s to 70s that Daumier wrote his own terse one-word titles. The writing seen on a few of the early proofs is that of Philipon, his co-editor Huart, and, in exceptionally rare cases, of Daumier himself.

Most impressions are ones that appeared in *Charivari* with the text on the verso. There are some impressions on white paper, but this is not always a guarantee that the lithography is superior. A further word of caution to collectors should be noted: there exist so-called proofs without letters, which have false margins — i.e. paper placed over the legends and proofs pulled to simulate proof before letters. The exceptional condition of most of the prints in the exhibition is the result of careful, scientific conservation.

Daumier drew his early lithographs directly on the stone without preparatory drawings. Towards the 1850s the quality of French newspaper deteriorated. In 1851 a process was patented by Firmin Gillot in which the image was engraved on a zinc plate by mechanical transfer. This relief process (called "gillotage") was adopted by printers of *Charivari* as a way to reproduce Daumier's images more readily. The greasy blacks of lithographs pulled directly from stones were lost, and pale grey, attenuated lines appear instead. The quality of the drawing remained autographic. The rarity of certain lithographs was not caused so much by connoisseurs or collectors of Daumier's graphic art as by the fact that certain pictures, when they appeared, had an instantaneous visual appeal. This is still true today. The bound volumes of *Charivari* and *La Caricature* are generally locked up in rare bookcases in public libraries to prevent vandalism. Even reissues of the most popular series, *Les Gens de Justice*, *Les Bons Bourgeois*, *Les Bas-Bleus* and others are often quickly mutilated by modern amateur collectors. The magic of the master appears irresistible.

A note on recent acquisitions: there are several works in the paintings, drawings and watercolors section of the catalogue which do not strictly follow other entries in numerical sequence but which are identified as recent acquisitions by an asterisk and a note on the page.

Any compiler of the monumental work of Daumier is so indebted to countless writers that to single out any author for special mention would be fatuous. The brief comments written under the entries are merely personal remarks intended only to stimulate the viewer to search for himself any number of other levels of interpretation or appreciation of Daumier's work.

Elizabeth Mongan

Lithographs

J'suis d'Garde à la mairie. — non ille de quisquam impune tulisset
Obvius armato! — Virgil

To shield your harvest, & defend your fire. .

1

J'SUIS D'GARDE À LA MERRIE (sic)
On guard at the Town Hall

Del. B, unique state, hand colored
1822

One of the first known lithographs made by Daumier when he was only fourteen years old. It was printed by Engelmann. Two inscriptions appear on the print: the first in Latin, *Non illi quisquam obvius armato impune tuliferit (sic)* Virgil; the other in English, "Shield your bravest and defend your fair." They do not seem to have any special relevance to the print. According to Delteil, impressions of these prints made in Daumier's youth are extremely rare.

2

PASSE TON CHEMIN, COCHON
Out of the way, pig

Del. 1, first state
LA SILHOUETTE, 22 July 1830

It is reminiscent of the work of Raffet, both in the subject, an imaginary scene connected with Napoleonic legends, and the treatment of shadowy light-grey lithographic tones. The lithograph was published by Ratier and signed in the lower right "Daumier."

3

DES VICTIMES DE LA RÉVOLUTION
"Comme c'est amusant la Politique."
Victims of the Revolution. Aren't politics funny.

Del. 14, second state
LA SILHOUETTE, 24 October 1830

Daumier probably made his first lithographs at the age of fourteen when he was a junior clerk for a deputy sheriff in Paris. His work, running around the streets of Paris as an errand boy, easily gave him the opportunity to observe the windows of print- and book-sellers, which at the time were filled with examples of Senefelder's new medium — lithography. Delpêch, on the Quai Voltaire, opened his printshop in 1816. Godefrey Engelmann, 18 Rue Cassette, and Comte Philibert de Lastreyrie, 8 Rue Saint-Marc, had preceded Delpêch in the sale of lithographs. Since Daumier's house in the Ile St. Louis was situated near most of the print-sellers, he could not fail to observe at an early age the work of Charlet, Bellange, Boilly, Géricault and many others. This lithograph was published in *La Silhouette* in 1830 when Daumier was twenty-two.

Passe ton chemin cochon.

Des Victimes de la Révolution.

Comme c'est amusant la politique

Clubert, Éde du journal la Caricature, (Au Magasin de Caricatures, Galerie Vero-dodat,   Lith. de Delaunois.

UN HÉROS DE JUILLET,
Mai 1831.

4

PAUVRES MOUTONS. AH! VOUS AVEZ
beau faire... Toujours on vous tondra
Poor sheep. Oh, you struggle in vain, you will always be shorn.

Del. 18, first state, hand colored
LA CARICATURE, deposited 1 December 1830

The lithograph represents the King, Louis-Philippe, shearing his unfortunate subjects. It was one of Daumier's earliest attacks on Louis-Philippe, and it appeared in the first issue of *La Caricature*, the journal founded and edited by Charles Philipon. The present colored impression is an early proof preceding the words *Caricatures Politiques* and the number.

5

UN HÉROS DE JUILLET. MAI 1831.
A hero of July. May 1831.

Del. 23, second state, hand colored
LA CARICATURE, deposited 1 June 1831

A despondent hero of the Revolution of July 1830 (which placed Louis-Philippe on the throne of France) meditates on his final step. Pawn tickets on his back, he stands solemnly on the balustrade of the Pont de la Concorde. The Chamber of Deputies, with the tri-color flying atop the famous colonnade, is seen to the right. The soft greys of the lithograph are in the manner of Charlet; the surety of drawing of the central figure already prefigures the evolving mastery of Daumier.

6

MONSEIGNEUR...NOUS METTRONS PARIS
en état de siège
Sir...we will put Paris under siege

Del. 24, unique state, hand colored
LA CARICATURE, deposited 1 June 1831

This lithograph and a companion piece, "Monseigneur, s'ils persistent..." were published as single sheets by the well-known editor of lithographs, Aubert. In May 1831 many protests took place in the Place Vendôme near the Obelisk. The Government was apprehensive that the protests might evolve into riots.

7

DIEU, AI-JE AIMÉ CET ÊTRE-LÀ
Lord, how I loved him

Del. 29, first state
LA CARICATURE, deposited 21 October 1831

Here is one of the most poignant of Daumier's early, rare lithographs. It already shows Daumier's prescience. It is simple and direct. The message of disillusionment must have been clear to the Parisians. All his life, Daumier was a journalist of the eye. He transformed what he felt into images that could be understood at once. A former National Guardsman with drooping shoulders is seen looking at the sculptured head of Louis-Philippe, who had been his idol!

Gargantua.

8

GARGANTUA

Del. 34, second state
LA CARICATURE, deposited 15 December 1831

The publication of this daring image of the Citizen King as a Rabelaisian giant gained instant notoriety for the young artist. Impressions of this print are now very rare, since it was seized and not published in *Charivari*. Daumier was not scatological, but here the drawing of the pierced chair made him liable to both a fine and six months' imprisonment in the Ste. Pélagie.

9

CONFÉRENCE DE LONDRES
London Conference

Del. 35, second state, hand colored
CARICATURES POLITIQUES, deposited 9 February 1832

A conference was held in London in 1832. At issue were the boundaries between Belgium and Holland. Casimir Périer was Minister of Foreign Affairs, and Talleyrand, then 78 years old, was Ambassador to London. Although the Ambassador was pro-English, he was not intemperate in his views. He wrote, "at every epoch, there is some good to be done or some harm to prevent; that is why, if one loves his country, in my opinion, one ought to serve it under all governments that it adopts."

10

NOUS N'AVONS PAS LA CROIX, NOUS
We don't have a medal

Del. 38, second state
LA CARICATURE, deposited 14 July 1832

This has much the same feeling as Del. B and Del. 1.

11

LE CAUCHEMAR
The Nightmare

Del. 41, unique state
LA CARICATURE, 23 February 1832

Lafayette, the hero of the Polish and American revolutions, is here depicted supine on an Empire sofa, his distended stomach weighed down by an enormous pear. The head of Lafayette is close to the features of the General in the well-known portrait by Ary Scheffer painted in 1822. The engraver Jean Marie Leroux (1788-1870) made an engraving after the old portrait, one which was popular in France. The implication is that Lafayette's indigestion was caused by Louis-Philippe. The latter is seen in the small picture above the sofa, with Lafayette behind him. The scrap of paper in the General's hand was the King's project for the Hôtel de Ville. In the lower right, the lithograph is signed "Rogelin," a nickname for Daumier.

Conference de Londres

12

LA COUR DU ROI PÉTAUD
The Court of King Pétaud

Del. 49, third state, hand colored
LA CARICATURE, 23 August 1832

This ambitious colored lithograph was inserted into the 1832 issue of *La Caricature*. The "Court of King Pétaud" signifies in English, "Bedlam broken loose." Daumier is here ridiculing the court of Louis-Philippe and his ministers.

13

BENJAMIN DELESSERT — BENJAMIN DUDESSERT

Del. 59, unique state
LA CARICATURE, 27 June 1833

Benjamin Delessert was represented in the *Ventre Législatif* (See cat. no. 26-O). Daumier also made two lithographs of him, the one included here and another, a half-length figure. Both were drawn in 1833.

14

DOCTEUR PRUNELLE — M. PRUNE

Del. 60, unique state
LA CARICATURE, 27 June 1833

Dr. Clément-François-Victor Gabriel Prunelle appears in this full-length study, as well as in the *Ventre Législatif* and in a clay bust. Although he was an able administrator, Dr. Prunelle's unfortunate physical appearance made him an easy subject for caricature. See cat. nos. 26-G and 213.

15

P.P. ROYER-COLLARD — M. ROYER-COL...

Del. 68, unique state
LA CARICATURE, 22 August 1833

Pierre Paul Royer-Collard appears in the *Ventre Législatif*. Daumier had also made a bust of him. Cat. no. 214 (Fogg no. 29). According to the Fogg catalogue, in this lithograph he is seen "as a sort of scarecrow stupidly shuffling along, now empty of all ideas." See cat. no. 26-L.

16

COMTE DE KÉRATRY — M. KÉRATR.

Del. 70, second state
LA CARICATURE, 19 September 1833

The Fogg catalogue describes the lithograph: "Filled with affected grace, and in his ballet shoes resembling a character in the *Commedia dell' Arte*." Mr. Kératry is one of the most animated of these early portrait prints by Daumier. See cat. no. 26-P.

La Caricature *(Journal)* N°152.

Pl. 319.

Ah! tu veux te frotter à la presse!!

L. de Becquet, rue Furstemberg 6.

chez Aubert, galerie vero dodat.

17

AH! TU VEUX TE FROTTER À LA PRESSE!!

Ah! You would meddle with the press!!

Del. 71, unique state
LA CARICATURE, 3 October 1833

The exact drawing of the large hand press is really the main concern of Daumier.
It is a symbol of real power. The vigorous workman with a cap indicating that
he is employed by the newspaper, *National*, and the most unfortunate King crunched
between the levers are reminders that a free press should not be stifled again, as it
was under the former restrictive laws of Charles X.

18

ADOLPHE JOLLIVET

Del. 75, unique state on china paper
LA CARICATURE, 27 December 1833

19

LE PASSÉ, LE PRÉSENT, L'AVENIR

The past, the present, the future

Del. 76, first state
LA CARICATURE, 9 January 1834

Louis-Philippe represented in three profiles. The caricature emphasizes the
hopelessness of the political climate — past, present and future: it is always the same.

20

BAISSEZ LE RIDEAU, LA FARCE EST JOUÉE

Lower the curtain, the comedy is over

Del. 86
LA CARICATURE, 11 September 1834

In this early masterpiece, Daumier has created a memorable image of the King. Seen
dressed as a clown standing at the proscenium of a theatre, he points to blind Justice
as the curtain slowly falls, covering with darkness the small, somnolent figures of
parliamentarians. The legend, probably added by Philipon, is from the well-known
phrase of Rabelais.

La Caricature (Journal) N° 164.

Pl. 346.

Chez Aubert, galerie vero dodat.

L. de Becquet rue Furstemberg 6.

M! JOLIV ...

La Caricature *(Journal)* N°. 166.

Pl. 349.

Le passé.   Le présent.   l'Avenir.

Chez Aubert, galerie vero dodat.

L. de Becquet, rue Furstemberg 6.

21

L'APOPLEXIE ALLANT REMPLACER
à Londres la paralysie

Apoplexy replaces paralysis in London

Del. 110, second state
LA CARICATURE, 26 February 1835

Two light carriages with folding hoods are seen passing each other. In one the aged, apoplectic Talleyrand is returning to Paris; in the other, the wizened, paralyzed Minister of Foreign Affairs, Marshal Sebastiani, lies in a semi-moribund state. He is on his way to London. It concludes Talleyrand's last mission after a lifetime of service to France. Born a nobleman in the eighteenth century, he was a power always to be reckoned with, whether on the stage in an official capacity or behind the scenes as an "eminence grise." Often controversial, Talleyrand's main policy was to seek accommodation, first with London and then, to balance the continental powers, with adroitness. He endorsed the Revolution, went into exile, returned to aid the Directory, advised Napoleon, and was consulted during the Restoration. A man of many parts, his main concern was always a secure France.

22

LE FANTÔME
The Phantom

Del. 115, first state
LA CARICATURE, 7 May 1835

The political trial of the leaders of the Republican uprising in Lyon (April 1834) opened in Paris on 5 May 1835. Daumier conjures up the specter of Napoleonic hero, Marshal Ney, condemned to death by the Bourbon Royalists in 1815 as a symbol of the current government's abuse of the law.

23

COMTE PORTALIS — DUC DE
Bassano — Comte de Montlosier

Del. 121, unique state
LA CARICATURE, 3 July 1835

24

HUGUET DE SÉMONVILLE — ROBERT
Macaire — (Thiers) — Comte Roederer

Del. 124, first state
LA CARICATURE, 30 July 1835

Pl. 488

Au bureau chez Aubert galerie Véro-Doda.

Lith. Delaunois rue du Boulai 19.

Le Fantôme.

GIROD DE L'AIN — J. JOSEPH
Rousseau — Amiral Verhuel

Del. 125, unrecorded state between second
and third, laid china paper
LA CARICATURE, 6 August 1835

Many of the liberals who had supported the July Revolution of 1830 were quickly
disillusioned by the "Citizen King." Some of the middle class, threatened by the
corruption and greed of the new ministry, began to seek an alliance with the
proletariat. Secret societies were formed, insurrection became endemic, and one group
of republicans was apprehended and brought to trial in the Luxembourg Palace in
April 1834. The judges at that infamous proceeding were selected from the Peers of
France. They were without exception men with a strong instinct for repressing any
tendency to reform existing inequities in society. Daumier drew the judges full-length
in a mock hierarchial stance to convey his contempt for their views. See cat. nos. 26,
27, 28 and 29.

LA CARICATURE (1830-1835) and CHARIVARI (founded in 1832)

Charles Philipon founded *La Caricature* in November 1830. It was a satirical paper with
pieces on politics, literature, travel and religion. Before it was suppressed in August of
1835, 251 issues containing 530 lithographs appeared. It came out every Thursday
with one page of text and two colored lithographs, which were inserted on loose
sheets. The text in the first issues was written by Balzac, who used a variety of
pseudonyms. Later texts were written by Louis Desnoyers. Despite their violence,
the texts were apparently considered less subversive than the lithographs.

In 1831 copies of the paper were confiscated nineteen times. Philipon was sentenced
to six months in prison and a fine of two thousand francs. Since Philipon had little
money, his friends came to his aid to pay this fine and many others. The caricaturist
Eugène Modeste Edmond Lepoitevin (1806-1870) proposed the idea of an album of
lithographs, which could be sold by Philipon to raise money. To meet the burden
of paying fines levied against *La Caricature*, Philipon published a series of single
lithographs. Daumier designed for *L'Association Mensuelle* five masterful lithographs,
which were issued singly. They were *Le Ventre Législatif* (The Legislative Belly); *Ne Vous
y Frottez Pas!* (Liberty of the Press); Enfoncé Lafayette! Attrapé Mon Vieux (Done For,
Lafayette); *Rue Transnonain*; and *Très Hauts et Très Puissants Moutards* (High and
Mighty Brats).

Charivari, an illustrated daily journal, was founded by Charles Philipon in 1832. When
La Caricature was suppressed, Philipon directed his energy to the sister publication.
When he was asked what the public could expect to find in *Charivari*, he replied with a
characteristic flow of words: "If it is not to be political, it will not be political: it will be
moral, literary, theatrical, artistic, social, medical, surgical, agricultural, somnambulist,
anabaptist, etc." This journal, to which Daumier contributed his lithographs,
continued to appear for more than thirty years.

LE VENTRE LÉGISLATIF.

Aspect des bancs ministériels de la chambre improstituée de 1834

LE VENTRE LÉGISLATIF
The legislative "belly"

Del. 131, unique state
L'ASSOCIATION MENSUELLE, January 1834

The celebrated print of *Le Ventre Législatif* was not drawn from life, as certain telling mannerisms of the characters might suggest. Rather the lithographic scene evolved over a period of time. It is known that Daumier was often in the Press Gallery and the *Salle des Pas Perdus* closely observing the members of the legislative body. From memory he modeled a series of clay busts of the Deputies (See cat. nos. 199-234). In these caricatures the witty deformations were often brutal. Next came a series of single caricatures, usually standing figures. These appeared in the *Charivari*. Finally a complete view of the chamber members was drawn on a lithographic stone. It is a devastating comment on the highest legislative body in France in 1833. Jean Adhémar, until recently the *Conservateur en Chef* of the *Cabinet des Estampes* in the Bibliothèque Nationale, has tentatively identified twenty-seven of the twenty-nine figures in the lithograph *Ventre Législatif*. The rest remain shadowy and unknown. The information about the individual deputies given here was taken from notes made by Adhémar and his staff many years ago for a catalogue which remained unpublished.

A. Guizot, François Pierre Guillaume
Born in Nîmes in 1787, died in 1874.

One of the great figures of the nineteenth century, Guizot was professor at the Sorbonne from 1812. Upon the return of Napoleon, he followed Louis XVIII into exile. From 1828 to 1830 he was Minister of the Exterior. Subsequently, he became Minister of Education and Minister of Foreign Affairs. Protestant, a man of high principle, Guizot was proud and rigid in his views. Often the target of the liberal press, Guizot, as shown here in profile, is solemn, thoughtful, and austere — a character not entirely unsympathetic to Daumier. See cat. no. 208.

B. Persil
Born in London in 1785, died in 1870.

The head of Persil appears half-hidden next to Guizot. Named General-Attorney by the Royal Court, Persil was a strong adversary of liberal ideas. He attacked the newspapers in numerous lawsuits against the press, litigations in which the jury often refused to follow him. He became Minister of Justice in 1834, when his vehemence against the press seemed to grow worse. In 1864, he became a senator. Daumier represented him often both in caricature and in one of the small sculptured busts. See cat. no. 226.

C. Thiers, Adolphe
Born in Marseilles in 1797, died in 1877.

Thiers' unusual physical appearance offered a marvelous opportunity to contemporary phrenologists. According to Lomenie, the shortness of his stature, the common expression of his features — half-hidden by enormous eyeglasses, the singular cadence of his accent, his continual jerkiness, the unevenness of his shoulders, and an absolute lack of manners, all contributed to produce "a being apart." His mental acumen was also ambivalent. An able politician and pupil of Talleyrand, he held a number of important ministerial positions, but his probity in financial matters was sometimes in doubt. Hippolyte Castille called him "Thiers the Jumper, a political Panurge." Nevertheless, it seems he was a man driven more by intellectual curiosity than ambition for power. He wrote ten volumes on the history of the Revolution and subsequently twenty more on the history of the Consulate and the Empire. Naturally, he was often in disagreement with Guizot. Thiers is the third figure in the first row.

D. Barthe, Félix

Born in Narbonne in 1795.

Barthe was born in Narbonne to a bourgeois family. Educated in Toulouse, he began his career as a liberal. He was highly esteemed as a young lawyer in Paris. At that time he made a specialty of defending writers and newspapers against attacks for their liberal views. Notably, he defended Béranger. In 1830 he became Minister of Education. From that time on, he became resolutely conservative. Louis-Philippe naturally was very happy with this evolution and defended Barthe against Guizot, saying "He is not a turncoat. He has been converted, he has seen the light." But for the caricaturists in the liberal press, it was an opportunity to emphasize his squint eyes, eyes which could not see clearly and thus led to conduct which was often equivocal and ambiguous. He was a survivor. In 1837 he was Minister of Justice and later Vice-President of the Chamber of Paris. He was out of office after the 1848 Revolution but was again elected to the Chamber in 1849. He was named Senator in 1852 by Napoleon III, who held him in high regard. See cat. no. 200.

E. Soult, Nicolas

Born in 1769 in St. Amans-la-Bastide in the province of Tarn.

The glum figure reading a document in the middle of the first row represents Soult. He was a politician and a famous general. An officer of the *ancien régime*, he distinguished himself in the Revolution and became Marshal of France in 1804. Later he fought in the great battles of Austerlitz, Eylau and Friedland, and was Major-General of the French army in the difficult Spanish War. There, it is said, he procured for himself a very fine collection of Spanish paintings. Banished by Louis XVIII, he reappeared in 1819 and was again, by Louis-Philippe, seated as a Peer of France in 1830. Balzac described him in *Cousine Bette* as "Maréchal, Prince de Wissembourg," aged seventy, with white hair, a tanned face and a forehead so vast it could be considered a battlefield. Journalists mocked his ignorance of grammar. See cat. no. 215.

F. D'Argout, Count Antoine Marie Apollinaire

Born at Château de Veyssilieux, Isère, in 1782.

D'Argout began his public career at the age of twenty-three as a clerk in the Department of Taxation. He took part in the Napoleonic wars, was made a Peer of France in 1814, and later rallied to the Restoration. During his long career he was Minister in turn of the Navy, Commerce, Public Works and Fine Arts, as well as Governor of the Bank of France, a post he held until his death in 1851. Vapereau summed up the career of d'Argout with the following formula, "He was always at ease with *pouvoir* (providing for himself)." An amusing comment by Balzac recounts how one night the nose of d'Argout was seen emerging from the gates of the Tuileries one minute and thirty-five seconds before the rest of his person. But d'Argout was also ridiculed because, as Minister of Fine Arts, he knew so little about painting. He was ignorant not only of the dates of famous artists but even of their names. The *National* published a squib in which a collector offered him a Rembrandt. D'Argout wrote in the margin of the letter, "make me a report, and tell me the various pictures that M. Rembrandt has sent to recent exhibitions of contemporary art." Another comment was, "Who is M. Ingres?" Daumier made a number of caricatures of d'Argout, as a figure standing in bronze. D'Argout for three or four years was the best subject for the caricaturists. His extraordinary nose was first described in prose by Balzac in 1832 in an article in *La Caricature* entitled "A Day With the Nose of M. d'Argout." "Of all the events connected with the July Revolution, one conspicuous fact unquestionably stands out as first rank, it is the nose of M. d'Argout." An amusing number of witticisms on the phenomenal nose quickly followed Balzac's lead. "M. d'Argout, despairing of finding a snuff box in harmony with his nose, is reduced to taking his tobacco in a chest..." "This nose, visible everywhere like the dome of the Invalides, is going to be left to a museum." See cat. no. 199.

G. Prunelle, Clément
Born in 1774, died in 1853.

The standing figure next to d'Argout is Clément Prunelle. Prunelle was a man of versatility. He was Professor of Medicine at Montpellier, Chief of Staff at Val de Grâce (as deputy from Isère), and later Mayor of Lyons. He is said to have worked fifteen to seventeen hours a day. His many interests, aside from his political career, included the study of architecture and research in libraries of France for unknown manuscripts. Among his many discoveries, the most unusual was a group of letters from Poussin to the Abbé Nicaise. The King held him in high regard. Dr. Prunelle was eloquent and witty in conversation. His unfortunate physique, however, made him a natural target for the caricaturists. His walk was cumbersome, his face round and commonplace; he had a very pronounced nose, little eyes hidden in deep sockets, thick lips (habitually pressed down), and a large square head covered with untidy, ugly hair, which made one critic call him "the bison." Since his ability was real and his smile luminous, the remark of a contemporary fashionable woman is of some value, "The more one observes Mr. Prunelle, the less one sees his face." See cat. nos. 14 and 213.

H. Fulchiron, J. Claude
Born in 1774, died in 1831.

The next to the last figure from the right in the front row is J. Claude Fulchiron. Daumier has drawn him with rather a silly grin on his face. Fulchiron was elected Deputy from Lyon in 1831. He always concurred with the Minister, rarely took his seat in the Chamber, and was generally considered to be a somewhat effectual busybody. See cat. no. 218.

I. Henry Gauthier, Count de Rigny
Born in 1782, died in 1835.

Gauthier was a nephew of Baron Louis de Rigny, to whom he owed his political appointment. He was made Minister of the Navy in 1831. *La Caricature* judged him severely, writing, "He was considered to be a great sailor by the newspaper, 'Le Constitutionnel,' a reputation he acquired at Navarino thanks to our sailors, but in the ports like Brest, they take a dim view of him." (In October of 1827 a combined fleet of English, French and Russian forces defeated an Egyptian-Turkish flotilla in Pylos Bay in the southwest Peloponnesus. In modern times, new Pylos is known as Navarino.) Daumier drew him standing (Del. 72) as well as in profile.

J. Podenas, Joseph, Baron de
Born in 1782, died in 1838.

Podenas was a political figure of minor importance. As a deputy in 1831 he voted with the extreme left, but after 1833 he was converted and became conservative. Daumier and Philipon transcribed his name, Pot-de-Noz, into "Pot Nose." The clay model of the deputy, though only 20.3 cm high, was described in the Fogg catalogue as "massive Podenas is the mightiest of Daumier's sculptures."
See cat. no. 216.

K. Harlé, Père, Jean Marie
Born 1763, died 1838.

Harlé was born into a farming family of Ardres. He became Comptroller for Calais and then for Upper-Marne, and finally Comptroller-General for Calais until 1812. From 1816 to his death, he was deputy for Calais. Until 1830 he voted with the liberals, Foy and Périer; after 1830, with the most independent of the conservatives, center left. The caricature of 8 June 1833 ranked him among the legislators who were gouty, ill-humored, asthmatic, rheumatic and arrogant. In 1830 Harlé was in fact sixty-seven years old. His son, Harlé, Jr., who succeeded him in the Chamber in 1838, had no more capacity, energy or independence than his father. See cat. no. 209.

L. Royer-Collard, Pierre Paul
Born in Sompuis in 1763, died at his property Château Vieux in 1845.

His mother, a Jansenist, supervised the early education of Royer-Collard. The Brothers of Christian Doctrine at Chaumont, where he studied, indoctrinated him with their principles. Napoleon appointed him Professor of the History of Philosophy at the École Normale. In 1819 he supported in vain the liberty of the press. After the revolution of 1830, Louis-Philippe named him Vice-President of the Chamber, but Royer-Collard refused to take his seat, and for four years he did not speak in the assembly. In 1835, he spoke openly against the press. After 1838, Royer-Collard retired to his country estate where he received his friends, notably Talleyrand and Guizot, giving them useful advice. His official biographer, A. Philippe, in 1857 painted a dismal picture of his subject: austere, obdurate, unable to bear contradiction, thrifty and neither charitable nor obliging. Furthermore, Royer-Collard inflicted on his family a way of life that was harsh and without joy. He spoke in a grave voice and wrote with difficulty because he was habitually lazy. Nevertheless, he had a certain spark and easily coined dreadful words that were later attributed to Talleyrand. Royer-Collard also had some curious whims: for years he could use only large colored cotton handkerchiefs (called *madras*), which he bought in the provinces. In 1808, at the age of forty-five, when he lost his hair (which he had powdered), he bought a wig that he sometimes wore backwards, giving his face a curious effect. His tufted eyebrows, long triangular nose and thick lips often made him appear menacing. Daumier represented him many times: in full-length, in one of the sculptured busts and in an early caricature (Del. 68) with a little deformation of features. See cat. nos. 15 and 214.

M. Odier, Antoine
Born in Geneva in 1766, died in Paris in 1853.

The politician Odier was son of a famous Swiss doctor. As a young man he was engaged in the export business of one of his relatives and spent some time in the

Orient. Later he was at Ostend and then Hamburg. He founded, in Alsace, a factory for the manufacture of printed calicos. For eleven years he was President of the Chamber of Commerce. He was elected Deputy in 1827. Louis-Philippe named him Peer of France in 1837. The Biography of Deputies said that his patriotism was doubtful and that he thought more of his fortune than his country. Daumier represented him twice exactly the same, once at full-length in a lithograph and once in a portrait bust (Fogg 24). Wearing eyeglasses, his hands folded, with a pugnacious expression on his face, he is seen as the fourth figure from the left in the second row in the *Ventre Législatif*. See cat. no. 211.

N. Fruchard

Nothing is definitely known of the gross figure seated in the second row next to Delessert. The *Charivari* called him very obscure: "His name so unknown that the most intense research has been unable to discover from which town M. Fruchard was elected deputy." The sculptured bust heightens the unattractive features of this unheard-of delegate. He was given a certain immortality, however, by Daumier and Philipon. See cat. no. 222.

O. Delessert, Benjamin
Born in Lyon in 1773, died in Paris in 1847.
Politician and manufacturer.

An officer in the artillery at the time of the Revolution, Delessert left the army for business. In 1801 he established the first cotton spinning mill in France. He also started a beet sugar factory, for which he was named a baron. Banker, regent of the Bank of France and president of the Court of Commerce, he was also elected deputy for the departments of Maine and Loire. From 1817 until 1824 he was a liberal; reelected in 1830, he became conservative. Daumier represented Delessert several times. In the bronze figure he is shown with a surpassing ugliness, his eyes almost sunken into the cranium and with a truncated nose. In the *Ventre Législatif*, the last figure on the second rank, he is seen to be a little more human, his nose a round protuberance on a disagreeably lined face. See cat. no. 217.

P. Kératry, Auguste Hilarion de
Born in Rennes in 1769, died in Paris in 1859.
Politician and author (man of letters).

After studying law at Quimper, Kératry went at the age of twenty-one to Paris. There he associated with two literary figures, Legouve and Bernardin de St. Pierre. He wrote romantic novels and philosophical treatises. In 1822 he completed three volumes on the *Beautiful in Art (Du Beau dans les Arts d'Imitation)*. In that document, he expounded at great length that "The real is the final condition of beauty in the arts." He admired the French school from David to Ingres to Géricault. During the Restoration he was deputy for Finisterre. At the time, he was left of center. Later, when again elected from 1849-52, he became suddenly very reactionary. Daumier drew a witty caricature of him in the full-length lithograph Del. 70 (See cat. no. 16). In the *Ventre* he appears on the third row, third from the left. See cat. nos. 16 and 219.

Q. Jollivet, Adolphe
Born in Berne in 1799, died in Paris in 1848. Lawyer.

Jollivet was elected to the Chamber of Deputies in 1830. He was noted for his good judgment, independence and loyalty to the Monarchy. By 1834 he changed his views and became intransigent. He voted for the law against the press. After 1839 he became concerned with colonial affairs. He was killed in the Tuileries in the Revolution of 1848. He appears in the *Ventre Législatif* in profile, seated next to Kératry in the third row.

R. Montalivet, Marthe Camille, Comte de Bachasson
Born in Valence in 1800, died in 1880. Politician.

Son of a Minister of the Interior under Napoleon who was Comptroller for the Emperor during the One Hundred Days. He succeeded his father as a Peer of France in 1823. In 1830 he became Minister of the Interior. As Comptroller for the Civil List after 1833, because of the parsimony of the King, Montalivet was the target of endless jokes. The caricature stated, "Mr. de Montalivet has been made a kitchen drudge; he has the portfolio of the scullery." Daumier drew him as *le charenton ministériel* (Del. 41), as a pastry cook (Del. 137), then on horseback (Del. 221) and finally on the throne of the King (Del. 118). In the Museum at Versailles there is a painting of him by Ary Schaeffer. He appears in the *Ventre Législatif* as the first figure at the left in the fourth row.

S. Barbé-Marbois, François, Marquis de
Born in Metz in 1745, died in 1837.

Barbé-Marbois was a Consul General in the United States, serving as Commissioner of St. Domenico (Caribbean). He returned to France in 1787. He took part in the Revolution. Deported to Guayana, he was recalled and was entrusted with the Louisiana Purchase. In 1808 he first became President of the Chamber of Accounts, then Senator. Louis XVIII made him a Minister of Justice. At the age of eighty-nine he presided at the trial of "The Accused of April" at the Luxembourg in 1834. In 1836 he wrote his autobiography. He was senile when later he was carried into the Chamber in his sick-chair. He is thought to be represented in the *Ventre Législatif* as the first figure in the third row, his aged head sunk onto his chest.

T. Viennet, Jean Pons Guillaume
Born in Béziers in 1777, died in 1868.
Politician, man of letters, army officer.

Until the Restoration, Viennet had a military career. He was twice taken prisoner by the English. Napoleon decorated him on the battlefield of Lutzen. In 1830 he was one of the first to hail Louis-Philippe. In 1831 he was made member of the French Academy. He became Peer of France in 1840. He was especially pleased with the July Monarchy and fought the Romantics in the name of the great classicists. Above all he was for order, and explained why: "I wish for tranquility for the state, because mine depends on it." He was most unpopular because of his attacks against the press. In fact, he made many enemies. He was excessively frank and spoke with a southern accent. Called "Golden Mouth," he said whatever came into his head. He was aware of his unpopularity and complained, "Five hundred epigrams are discharged against me, against my face, my cowlick, my green frock-coat." He was often ridiculed in *La Caricature*. Daumier made at least five

ENFONCÉ LAFAYETTE!....... ATTRAPPE, MON VIEUX !

caricatures of him, one of which was a sculptured bust. He is seen drawn by Daumier at the tribune in inclined profile with a hydrocephalic forehead (29 March 1833, Del. 145). See cat. no. 221.

U. Sebastiani, Count Horace

Born in Corsica in 1775, died in Paris.
General and statesman.

Sebastiani became one of the great generals of Napoleon, known for both his audacity and his elegance. It is said that during the campaign in Prussia his baggage was captured by the Cossacks, who believed it belonged to a milliner. In 1830, after some hesitation, he said the flag of Napoleon was the only one and that the deputies did not have the right to wear the tri-colored cockade. He switched to Louis-Philippe. The latter named him Minister of Foreign Affairs. Subsequently he replaced Talleyrand at the court in London. *Charivari*, in an article 6 December 1833, declared Sebastiani "Minister of Nothing, entirely abreast of his functions." A foppish old man, he hardly entered the Chamber after 1834 and then only to drink at the bar, talk nonsense at the rostrum and doze in his place. He retired in 1847 when his daughter, the Duchess of Prasline, was murdered by her husband. He was interred in the Invalides by order of Napoleon III. He is to be seen in the *Ventre Législatif* in the third row, the third figure on the right. His features also correspond to those in the sculptured bust which Daumier made of him. See cat. no. 228.

27

NE VOUS Y FROTTEZ PAS
Don't meddle around

Del. 133, unique state
L'ASSOCIATION MENSUELLE, March 1834

In the foreground a defiant printer is seen with his feet planted firmly before the words "Liberty of the Press." To his left an impatient king strides forward to attack the press, pushed by Persil but restrained by Thiers. To his right is a cautionary tale of the former King Charles X, who was brought down by his restrictive policies.

28

ENFONCÉ, LAFAYETTE!...ATTRAPÉ, MON VIEUX!
Done for, Lafayette! Trapped, old fellow!

Del. 134, unique state
L'ASSOCIATION MENSUELLE, May 1834

On a rocky mound an obese figure of a man dressed in mourning, his hands clasped in prayer, bows his head in seeming grief. Behind him to the left a funeral cortege followed by a large crowd moves slowly towards Père Lachaise Cemetery. The massive central figure represents the King, Louis-Philippe. The funeral is that of General Lafayette.

After the July Revolution, Lafayette hailed Louis-Philippe as King of the French. The General was then named, by the Provisory Government, Commandant of the National Guard, the rank he had held in 1789 when the Revolution began. In December of 1830, the King abolished the Guard. Lafayette was dismissed without pay. He returned to his seat in the Chamber as a liberal, strongly opposed to the new restrictive policies of the King. Lafayette died in 1834.

RUE TRANSNONAIN, LE 15 AVRIL 1834

Types Français. 2

Au bureau chez Aubert, gal. Véro Dodat. Lith. Junca.

charivari 27-7bre 1835

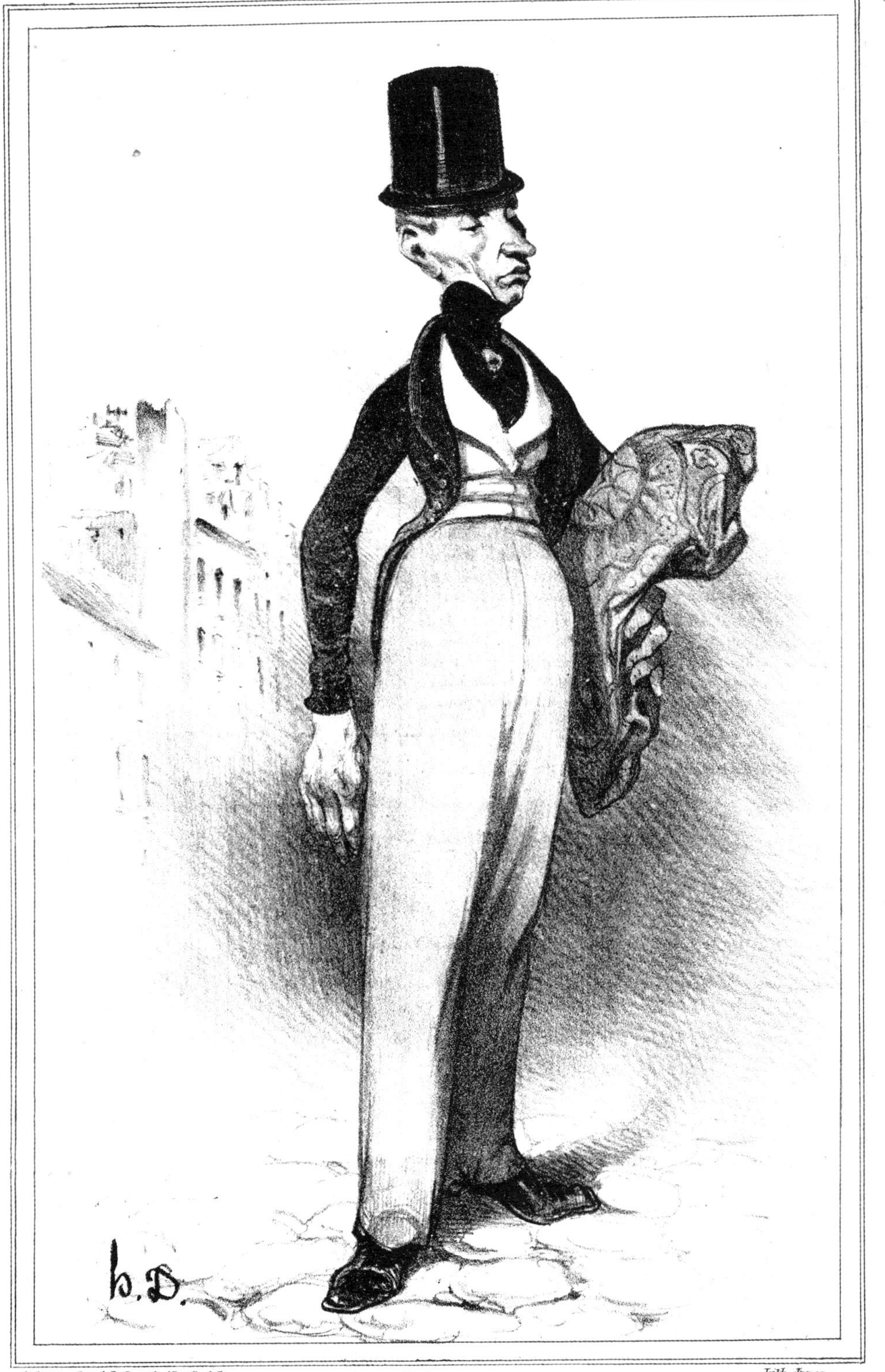

Le Tailleur,

Il marche cambré, les épaules en porte-manteau et les coudes en dehors. Ses habits, coupés dans le dernier genre, jurent souvent avec ses bottes et son chapeau, il a

Daumier's tribute to the great General is evident in this portrayal of his solemn funeral. The romantic landscape in the background was drawn by Paul Huet (1803-1869).

29

RUE TRANSNONAIN, LE 15 AVRIL 1834
Transnonain Street, the 15th of April, 1834

Del. 135, unique state
L'ASSOCIATION MENSUELLE, July 1834

Champfleury, writing in the *History of Modern Caricature*, said "Everyone remembers this terrible drama. Because of it the word 'Transnonain' remains sinister." In the early 1830s, riots often broke out in the working quarter of St. Martin in Paris. On the 15th of April an insurrection was put down with wanton brutality by the government soldiers. An innocent family in a modest house was murdered. There were many published depositions by eyewitnesses of the affair, here made explicit by Daumier in a realistic, graphic statement which in its dark modernity still has the power to shock.

30

LA FAMILLE D'ARGOUT PENDANT L'ORAGE
The d'Argout family during the storm

Del. 165, second state
CHARIVARI, 29 September 1833

Here is another droll depiction of the celebrated nose of the Count d'Argout. As d'Argout strolls with his family in a downpour of rain, the nose serves as a marvelous umbrella. Daumier even allowed himself a touch of poignancy describing the charming little girl protected by her father in the inclement weather.

31

LE TAILLEUR
The Tailor

Del. 261, second state
CHARIVARI, 27 September 1835

An example of Daumier's ability to capture the sense of style among the tradespeople of the city, this illustration gives an indication of his later fascination with the theater. Here a single figure suggests in mime a small drama.

32

L'AMATEUR D'HUÎTRES
The Oyster Connoisseur

Del. 329, second state
CHARIVARI, 7 December 1836

This is a delicious commentary on the gourmet pretensions of the middle class. More important, Daumier here indulges himself artistically a little. His private avocation at the time was a study of cranial structure as a clue to personality, a study influenced by Lavater's theories.

L'amateur d'huîtres.   The Lover of oisters.

329

Robert Macaire professeur d'industrie.

Exemple: Vous achetez un produit nouveau, n'importe quel bon ou mauvais, vous l'achetez 600 f._ 300 f._ 25 francs le moins. C... possible! Vous avez 300,000 f. d'actions le plus possible! Vous faites des annonces-monstre, des affiches monstre, des prospectus-monstre, vous réussis; le capital, vous l'empochez vous mettez ensuite la clé sous la porte vous déposez votre bilan c'est-à-dire ... de ... de la monde ... Et ... fait et vous faites d'un autre.

ROBERT MACAIRE

Since Daumier had an unfailing instinct for the telling gesture and the dramatic moment, it is not surprising that he took a special delight in the theater. In a melodrama, *À L'Auberge des Adrets* (published in 1823), the popular actor Frederick Lemaître gave a highly successful portrayal of a dandy called "Robert Macaire." Between 1836 and 1838, Daumier designed one hundred pictures of the charlatan, always accompanied by his straight man, a skinny dead-pan character named "Bertrand." Philipon invented the episodes and provided the legends. Together they captured through social comment the political ethos of Louis-Philippe's reign.

The series, under the name "Caricaturana," appeared in the *Charivari*. Later the same images were published in book form by Aubert, with expanded texts by Louis Huart and Maurice Alhoy.

33

ROBERT MACAIRE, PHILANTHROPE
Vois-tu Bertrand nous faisons de la morale
en actions.

Robert Macaire, Philanthropist
Look, Bertrand — we will manipulate morally the stock
market shares.

Del. 355, third state
Caricaturana
CHARIVARI, 28 August 1836

The wall of the building in the background is plastered with posters advertising stocks for sale. Robert Macaire, with one hand on the shoulder of Bertrand, is seen demonstrating a new hare-brained scheme to get rich quick.

34

ROBERT MACAIRE, PROFESSEUR D'INDUSTRIE
Robert Macaire, Professor of Industry

Del. 377, third state, hand colored
Caricaturana
CHARIVARI, 29 January 1837

Here Robert Macaire, dressed in academic garb, is lecturing a fascinated audience on his far-reaching economic theories. The industrial revolution was well under way in France. Some gullible people were taken by an obsession with the new mercantile boom.

35

LE PUBLIC, MON CHER...EST STUPIDE
The public, my dear, is stupid

Del. 425, second state
Caricaturana
CHARIVARI, 24 December 1837

Here Robert Macaire, as a doctor, is seen in the foreground. In the background a funeral procession of shadowy figures winds slowly through the city streets. The text

Le public, mon cher, le public est stupide.... nous le saignons à blanc, nous le purgeons à mort, il n'est pas content.... il veut du nouveau... donnons lui en morbleu du nouveau, faisons nous homoeopates.... il aime les blagues, traitons le par ses semblables Similia Similibus (Bertrand Amen. Tiens voici une ordonnance qui résume le système. Prendre un tout petit grain de De rien du tout. Le couper en dix millions de molécules jeter une une seule de ces dixmillionnièmes parties dans la rivière... remuer, remuer triturer beaucoup.. laisser infuser quelques heures. puiser un seau de cette eau bienfaisante la filtrer la couper avec 20 parties d'eau ordinaire et en humecter la langue tous les matins à jeun.. Voilà!
— Est ce tout ? — Oui Ah! diable! j'oubliais le principal.. Payer la présente ordonnance.

explains that since the public is stupid, "We will bleed them white — we will purge them to death...." The fine print contains a recipe for a new cure made from a grain of nothing at all pounded into millions of molecules.

36

CRIE DONC, MÂTIN...

Scream, Kid...

Del. 467, second state
Croquis d'Expressions
Sketches of Expression
CHARIVARI, 6 February 1838

This lithograph of a monstrous crying child and the two following prints are from a little-known series that was published in *Charivari* called "Sketches of Expressions." The meaning is inherent in the drawing. Captions are unnecessary.

37

IL A DONC ÉTÉ BIEN MÉCHANT...

He has been very naughty...

Del. 470, first state
Croquis d'Expressions
Sketches of Expression
CHARIVARI, 28 February 1838

38

POUR ALLER JUSQU'AU COEUR...

To reach the heart...

Del. 516, second state
Croquis d'Expressions
Sketches of Expression
CHARIVARI, 28 March 1839

39

PARADE DU CHARIVARI

Charivari Parade

Del. 554, second state
CHARIVARI, 6 January 1839

40

L'ODORAT

Smell, from the *Five Senses*

Del. 594, fourth state
Types Parisiens
Parisian Types
LA CARICATURE, 21 July 1839
CHARIVARI, 18 January 1843

An old bachelor in his cotton nightcap is seen in the early morning light, savoring a very small blossom. The somewhat disheveled windowsill filled with herbs in pots is drawn with an inimitable verve. What a far cry are these two scenes from the representations of the Five Senses in older engravings of the sixteenth and seventeenth centuries! There is almost a double mocking: one on the theme, the other on the frail Parisian types.

41

LA VUE

Sight, from the *Five Senses*

Del. 595, third state
Types Parisiens
Parisian Types
LA CARICATURE, 4 August 1839
CHARIVARI, 14 September 1842

42

CE MATIN AVANT L'AURORE...

This morning before dawn...

Del. 627, third state, hand colored
Moeurs Conjugales
Married Life
CHARIVARI, 9 June 1839

A whimsical commentary on married life. The model for the father was Daumier himself.

43

VOILÀ LE MOMENT (PASSÉ MINUIT) OÙ LE CALME
et la paix règnent véritablement
dans les heureux ménages.
Vaut mieux tard que jamais.
Now is the time (past midnight) when peace truly
reigns in happy families. Better late than never.

Del. 652, second state
Moeurs Conjugales
Married Life
CHARIVARI, 22 November 1840

TYPES PARISIENS.

L'ODORAT.

TYPES PARISIENS.

39.

Imp. d'Aubert & Cie

LA VUE

22 nov. 1840

Imp d'Aubert & C.ie

Voilà le moment (passé minuit) , où le calme et la paix règnent véritablement dans les heureux ménages . Vaut mieux tard que jamais .

Se vend Chez Bauger & C.ie Editeurs des Dessins de la CARICATURE du FIGARO et du CHARIVARI Rue du Croissant N° 16

44

IL FAUT SEMER DE FLEURS LE CHEMIN DE LA VIE
One must scatter flowers on the path of life

Del. 709, second state
Émotions Parisiennes
Parisian Experiences
CHARIVARI, 2 February 1840

Daumier here is suggesting, with a fine Gallic irony akin to Voltaire's, that even in the best of all possible worlds it is necessary sometimes to scatter a few flowers.

45

C'EST UNIQUE! J'AI PRIS QUATRE TAILLES
juste comme celles — là dans ma vie...
What a coincidence! I have held four waists just like these in my life...

Del. 711, second state
Émotions Parisiennes
Parisian Experiences
CHARIVARI, 7 February 1840

46

INGRATE PATRIE TU N'AURAS PAS MON OEUVRE
Thankless country, you shall not have my work!

Del. 719, third state
Salon de 1841
Salon of 1841
LA CARICATURE, 15 March 1840

Throughout his long career as a commentator on human foibles, Daumier drew, periodically, mischievous pictures of the egotism of certain artists. This lithograph shows two artists dressed in contemporary Bohemian clothes, each reacting extravagantly to a situation. It is interesting that Daumier drew this picture a year before Baudelaire published his first critique on the Salons.

47

ÉQUITATION BOUTIQUIÈRE
Rented horses

Del. 754, second state
Les Parisiens
Parisians
CHARIVARI, 1 December 1839

EMOTIONS PARIENNES.

Chez Bauger R. du Croissant 16

Imp d'Aubert & C.ᵉ

Il faut semer de fleurs le chemin de la vie !..........

ACTUALITÉS

Chez Aubert gal Vero-Douat   imp d Aubert & Cie   Chez Banger R du Croissant 16

Ingrate patrie, tu n'auras pas mon œuvre!......

LES PARISIENS.

Equitation boutiquière sur des chevaux de louage, et où il n'y a pas autre chose à louer . . . .

48

LES BADAUDS

Bystanders

Del. 755, second state
Les Parisiens
Parisians
CHARIVARI, 5 December 1839

49

VOYAGE À ST. CLOUD

Trip to St. Cloud

Del. 765, second state
Les Baigneurs
The Bathers
CHARIVARI, 6 September 1839

The view on the Seine below Paris is barely indicated. In calm midstream two intrepid swimmers, their clothing in a barrel, seem quite unlikely to reach their destination, St. Cloud.

50

C'EST PRESQUE TOUJOURS À LA HALLE...

It's usually to the market...

Del. 816, proof before letters
La Pêche
Fishing
LA CARICATURE, 19 July 1840

(Upper margin)
On viendra prendre la lettre demain matin chez vous à onze h. De cette pierre;
Donnez-la svp avec d'autres, si c'est possible (à Zartino? M. Zartino?)
The inscription will be picked up at your place at 11 o'clock tomorrow morning. Of this stone; please give it along with others, if possible (to Zartino? M. Zartino?)

(Lower margin)
C'est presque toujours à la halle que les pêcheurs Parisiens vont attraper leur poisson.
It's usually to the market that Parisian fisherman go to catch their fish.

(Left margin)
Le compte pour celle-ci?
The charge for this one?

LES PARISIENS

LES BADAUDS.

On ne peut pas croire, il est impossible de croire que ce pauvre pêcheur perché sur un bateau soit le motif de ce rassemblement. A coup sûr, les parisiens cette caste intelligente et active, est clouée là par un évènement grave, une modiste pair de France, un M.d de marrons, un candidat à l'Accadémie, victime de l'amour ou de l'ambition!.... Eh bien non, c'est réellement un goujon que vous ne voyez pas et qu'ils ne voient pas non plus . . . . . .

LES BAIGNEURS.

Voyage à St Cloud.

LA PÊCHE.

L'EAU DU PUITS DE GRENELLE
-Décidément cette eau chaude est très mauvaise à boire.
-Oui, mais il y a beaucoup de petits insectes dedans.

Water from the springs of Grenelle.
-This warm water tastes awful.
-Yes, but it is so full of little bugs.

Del. 915, second state
Actualités
Current Events
LA CARICATURE, 14 March 1841
CHARIVARI, 21 March 1841

Two skeptics sampling water from the new artesian well in the Paris suburb of Grenelle. This is the second of four states. In the first two states (neither of which was published) the "s" was omitted from the word *puits.*

CHARMÉ DE SE VOIR EXPOSÉ
Delighted to be hung...

Del. 918, fourth state
Actualités
Current Events
LA CARICATURE, 25 April 1841
CHARIVARI, 2 May 1841

HISTOIRE ANCIENNE
Ancient History

At a time when the battle between classicism and romanticism was waged in painting, literature, music and the theater, all who were passionately interested in the arts became involved. Delacroix's famous question, "Who will deliver us from the Greeks?" could well have been Daumier's inspiration for his own contribution to the controversy. With subjects and captions chosen by scholar and writer Albéric Second, Daumier produced the series, *Histoire Ancienne.* In these, familiar subjects from Greek myths are presented in a startling new way. Pygmalion, Ulysses, Alcibiades, Endymion and Penelope, although dressed *à la grecque* are represented in utterly absurd situations.

PRESENTATION D'ULYSSE À NAUSICA
Introduction of Ulysses to Nausicaa

Del. 928, second state
Histoire Ancienne
Ancient History
CHARIVARI, 30 March 1842

ACTUALITES .

Chez Bauger R. du Croissant, 16

Imp. d'Aubert & Cᵉ

L'EAU DU PUIT DE GRENELLE .

– Décidement cette eau chaude est très mauvaise a boire
– Oui, mais il y a beaucoup de petits insectes dedans !

ACTUALITES.

Charmé de se voir exposé, l'original ici présent conduit son épouse au salon et la place devant son image pour jouir du jugement de la foule. – Tiens disent les uns c'est le Commissaire Chinois Lin ! – Non disent les autres vous ne voyez donc pas que c'est de l'histoire naturelle ! – C'est, reprend un Monsieur possesseur du livret, c'est le portrait de Mr D... courtier d'assurances. – Ah bon avec une boule comme ça il n'a pas besoin de s'assurer on ne l'enlèvera pas. Madame sa femme était seulement très flattée.

54

ULYSSE ET PÉNÉLOPE
Ulysses and Penelope

Del. 938, proof before letters
Histoire Ancienne
Ancient History
CHARIVARI, 26 June 1842

55

JEUNESSE D'ALCIBIADE
Alcibiades' Youth

Del. 943, unrecorded state between second and third
Histoire Ancienne
Ancient History
CHARIVARI, 17 July 1842

56

ENDYMION

Del. 969, second state
Histoire Ancienne
Ancient History
CHARIVARI, 21 December 1842

57

PYGMALION
"Oh triomphe des arts! Quelle fût ta surprise,
Grand Sculpteur, quand tu vis ton marbre s'animer,
et d'un air chaste et doux, lentement se baisser
pour te demander une prise (Comte Siméon)
Oh triumph of art! With what astonishment,
Great Sculptor, you must have seen your marble come alive,
And with chaste and gentle manner, slowly lean down,
To ask for a pinch of snuff (Comte Siméon)

Del. 971, second state
Histoire Ancienne
Ancient History
CHARIVARI, 28 December 1842

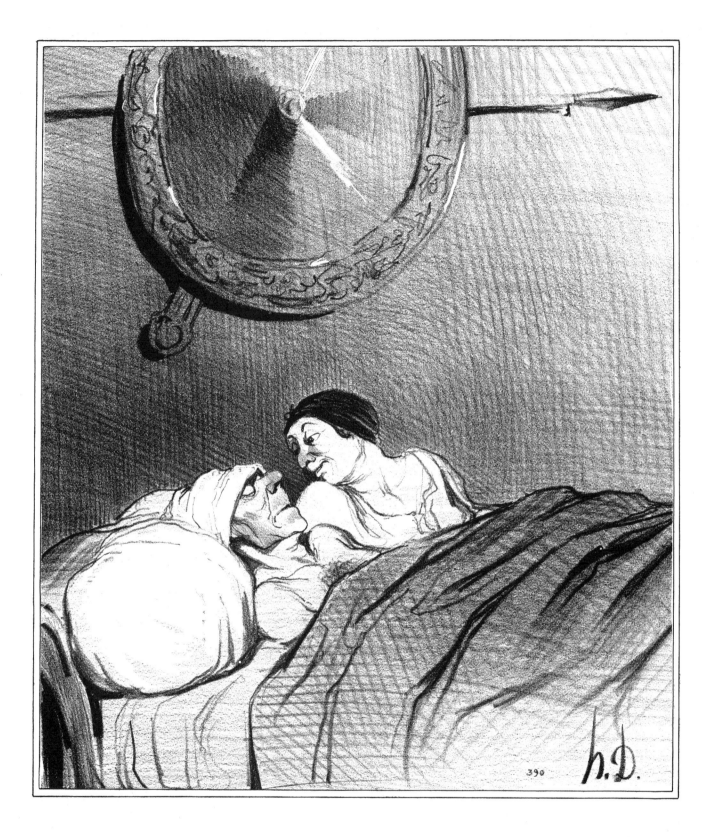

HISTOIRE ANCIENNE.

Chez Bauger. R. du Croissant, 16. Imp. d'Aubert. &C.

JEUNESSE D'ALCIBIADE.

Ce dandy rutilant, auréolé de fleurs,
Si crânement galbé dans sa prestance riche,
Voulant faire un beau jour la queue a ses blagueurs,
Coupa celle de son caniche.

Ballade grecque de Mr Théoph. Gautier.

HISTOIRE ANCIENNE.

47.

PYGMALION.

O triomphe des arts ! quelle fût ta surprise,
Grand sculpteur, quand tu vis ton marbre s'animer,
Et, d'un air chaste et doux, lentement se baisser
Pour te demander une prise.

(Comte Siméon.)

58

SCÈNES PARLEMENTAIRES

Parliamentary Scenes

Del. 1013, first state
Scènes Parlementaires
Parliamentary Scenes
CHARIVARI, April 1843, never published

Delteil recorded that there was a series of six pieces entitled *Scènes Parlementaires*, and that one of them, no. 4, did not exist. Five were published in *Charivari* in 1843. This recently discovered lithograph is without question the missing print Delteil had presumed to exist but had not seen, since it was never published. A handwritten notation in brown ink appears in the upper right corner of the print: "Numéro qui etait mis sur blanc, no. 4." (The image appeared as Del. 1013 with a censored caption and was also never published.)

The following handwritten legend is attached to the proof: "L'honorable M. Rigaudin va passer la nuit dans la Salle des Conférences afin de pouvoir le lendemain matin s'insérer le premier sur la liste des orateurs qui parlent contre ou pour le projet de la loi. Il va sans dire qu'il ne parle jamais." (The Honorable Mr. Rigaudin passing the night in the conference room to be sure that next morning he will be the first on the list to speak either for or against a point of law. It goes without saying that he will never speak.)

59

UNE RENCONTRE DÉSAGRÉABLE

Dangerous Encounter

Del. 1038, first state proof before letters
Les Canotiers Parisiens
Boating in Paris
CHARIVARI, 6 July 1843

In these airy prints the anecdote, as always, is arresting; more subtle is the ambiance and the freedom with which it is contrived. The three tones — grey, black and white — in the hands of an ordinary printmaker are fairly limited. In the boating series of the early forties, a series consisting of twenty lithographs, Daumier creates, as a great landscape painter would, the elusive quality of light.

LE JARDIN DES TUILERIES
-On ne fume pas ici Messieurs.
-C'est dans le jardin que vous voulez dire?
-Comment donc! Nous y avons fumés hier toute la
journée et on ne nous a rien dit!
The Tuileries Gardens
-No smoking here, Sir.
-You mean in the Gardens?
-What do you mean? We were here yesterday and
nobody said anything!

Del. 1071, second state
La Chapitre des Interprétations
Interpretations
CHARIVARI, 26 December 1843

This is a proof of the second state with a change of the legend in ink. Apart from being a characteristic stab at petty rules, Daumier has drawn here a charming corner of the Tuileries Gardens.

61

UNE PROMOTION
Approche Anastase...j'te vas réveler
les secrets du métier...
A Promotion
Come here, Anastase...I'm going to reveal the
secrets of the trade to you...

Del. 1145, second state
Les Beaux Jours de la Vie
Red Letter Days
CHARIVARI, 30 April 1845

The young apprentice has serious doubts about his future career as a chef.

62

QUAND ON A SON PORTRAIT AU SALON
One's portrait at the Salon

Del. 1147, third state
Les Beaux Jours de la Vie
Red Letter Days
CHARIVARI, 26 April 1845

Chez Aubert & Cie Pl. de la Bourse

Imp d Aubert & Cie

UNE PROMOTION.

- Approche, Anastase.... à partir d'aujourd'hui tu cesses d'être **gâte-sauce**, je t'élève à la dignité de cuisinier......
j'te vas révéler les secrets du métier...... et pour commencer tu vas apprendre comment avec un matou, l'on vous
fricotte un lapin, qu'on fait ensuite manger pour du lièvre !....

63

MANIÈRE CHINOISE DE NETTOYER LES
rues et de salir les passans (sic)
The Chinese way to clean the streets and soil the pedestrians

Del. 1220, second state
Voyage en Chine
Chinese Trip
CHARIVARI, 23 June 1845

Daumier here has created a bizarre street scene. Tall Chinese dressed in their native costumes are violently sloshing dirty pavement water while harried Parisians group for protection. Curiosity about the Far East was prevalent in Paris long before the famous Japanese Exhibition in 1867, but Daumier in his inimitable way has looked at the phenomenon of Orientalism and given a quite personal interpretation. Just as in the suite of *Histoire Ancienne*, here it is obvious foolishness to see Mandarins as sanitation agents.

64

ADIEU, MON CHER, JE VAIS CHEZ MES EDITEURS...
Goodbye, dear, I am going to my publishers'...

Del. 1223, third state
Les Bas-Bleus
Bluestockings
CHARIVARI, 8 February 1844

"Bluestocking" was an eighteenth century English word coined to describe a group of gentlemen who met at Montague House in London for literary discussions rather than to play cards. In defiance of an accepted code of dress, they wore blue worsted instead of black stockings. Across the Channel, in the early nineteenth century, it was translated as "Bas-Bleu" and was used to denigrate a new feminine movement. *La Femme Libre*, a newspaper for women, was founded by Jeanne Désirée in 1832. Other gifted women — Cécile Fournel, Suzanne Vailquin and Claire Demar — all inspired by Claude Henri de Rouvroy Saint-Simon, the nineteenth century Socialist, wrote with intelligence. That they were over-shadowed by Georges Sand and Flora Tristan does not lessen their contribution to the emancipation of women in France. Daumier, with his roving reportorial eye and understanding of human comedy, wherever it might appear, was entranced by the eruption of a colorful new species, the literary woman. Daumier's caricatures in the Bas-Bleu series were directed at pretentious, aggressive writers of limited capacity. In addition to *Les Bas-Bleus*, there are two other series: *Les Divorceuses* and *Les Femmes Socialistes* in which Daumier addresses himself to the question of the liberated woman.

VOYAGE EN CHINE.

Chez Aubert & C.ⁱᵉ Pl de la Bourse 29.

Imp. d'Aubert & Cⁱᵉ

MANIÈRE CHINOISE

DE NETTOYER LES RUES ET DE SALIR LES PASSANS.

LES BAS BLEUS.

Chez Aubert, Pl. de la Bourse, 29.   Imp. d. Aubert & Cie.

Adieu, mon cher, je vais chez mes éditeurs;.... je ne rentrerai probablement que fort tard...
ne manquez pas de donner encore deux fois la bouillie à Dodore.....s'il a besoin......d'autre
chose.... vous trouverez ça sous le lit....

65

LA MÈRE EST DANS LE FEU DE
la composition...
The mother, in the fever of creation

Del. 1227, second state
Les Bas-Bleus
Bluestockings
CHARIVARI, 26 February 1844

66

MONSIEUR, PARDON SI JE VOUS
gêne un peu...
Sorry, Sir, am I in your way?

Del. 1233, third state
Les Bas-Bleus
Bluestockings
CHARIVARI, 8 March 1844

67

ENTRE ONZE HEURES ET MINUIT
Sapristi! Voilà un homme qui a l'air
bien féroce... Je donnerai dix ans de la
vie de ma femme pour avoir un pistolet.
Between 11 o'clock and midnight
Dammit! The fellow looks dangerous...
I would give ten years of my wife's life
to have a pistol.

Del. 1329, first state, proof before letters with
hand written title and caption
Paris l'Hiver
Paris in the Winter
CHARIVARI, 21 December 1844

68

MANIÈRE INGÉNIEUSE DE DÉCHARGER LE
toits de neige, et en chargeant les passants
Ingenious means of clearing snow off the roofs and onto
pedestrians

Del. 1330, proof before letters with hand written
title and caption
Paris l'Hiver
Paris in Winter
CHARIVARI, 31 December 1844

LES BAS BLEUS.

Chez Aubert & Cⁱᵉ Pl. de la Bourse 29.

Imp. d'Aubert & Cⁱᵉ

— Monsieur, pardon si je vous gêne un peu.... mais vous comprenez qu'écrivant en ce moment un roman nouveau, je dois consulter une foule d'auteurs anciens !......

— (Le Monsieur à part.) Des auteurs anciens !.... parbleu elle aurait bien dû les consulter de leur vivant, car elle a dû être leur contemporaine !....

Paris l'hiver

Entre onze heures et minuit

Entre onze heures et minuit
— Saprist... Voilà un homme que j'ai bien ferace... ça doit
être un Chourineur... et je n'ai pas le moindre poignard.
— Saperlotte... que je suis perdu... il est impossible
que ce brigand ne soit pas un Escarpe... je donnerais
dix ans de la vie de ma femme pour avoir
un pistolet!...

*Manière ingénieuse de décharger les toits de
Neige en en chargeant les passants.*

ABONNÉES RECEVANT LEUR JOURNAL ET
cherchant la manière de s'en servir

Subscribers trying to cope with their morning paper

Del. 1335, second state
Actualités
Current Events
CHARIVARI, 31 January 1845

LES GENS DE JUSTICE

Men of Justice

Between March 1845 and October 1848 Daumier designed a celebrated series of
lithographs called the *Gens de Justice*. They were published in the *Charivari* with
the exception of two subjects. Daumier, like Rembrandt, was self-educated. His
development progresses steadily in the forties. In the set of lawyers, anecdotal detail
is less important than the movement of form under flowing black robes. The major
theme, victims of justice subjected to the special pleading of cynical lawyers, also
appears in a number of vivid watercolors, probably made at the same time.

M. LE JUGE DE PAIX A RENDU SA DÉCISION,
les parties sont censées conciliées.

*His honor has pronounced judgment, the parties are
presumed reconciled.*

Del. 1361, second state
Les Gens de Justice
Men of Justice
CHARIVARI, 24 October 1846

GRAND ESCALIER DU PALAIS DE JUSTICE,
vue de faces

Grand staircase of the Palace of Justice, front view
(The "s" in the word "faces" creates a pun meaning
"survey of faces.")

Del. 1372, third state
Les Gens de Justice
Men of Justice
CHARIVARI, 8 February 1848

Louis XIII 1610 - 1643

Philippe, duc d'Orléans
le Régent
Louis
Louis Philippe
Philippe - Egalité
Louis - Philippe I er (1830-48)
ep Marie-Amélie de Naples

Ferdinand, duc d'Orléans
Louise ep Léopold I er roi des Belges
François, prince de Joinville
Louis, duc d'Aumale
Henri
Antoine, duc de Montpensier

Louis, comte de Paris
Robert, duc de Chartres

Philippe, duc d'Orléans
Jean, duc de Guise

Henri, comte de Paris
né en 1908

Louis XIV 1643 - 1715

Louis, le grand dauphin
Louis, duc de Bourgogne
Louis XV 1715 - 1774
Louis, le dauphin
Louis XVI ep Marie Antoinette
Louis XVIII 1814 - 1824
Charles X 1824 - 1830

Louis XVII
Madame Royale

Duc d'Angoulême
Duc de Berry (assassiné en 1820)

Comte de Chambord
(Henri V)

LES GENS DE JUSTICE.

36.

Grand escalier du Palais de justice.
Vue de faces.

72

MA GREFFE D'UN CERISIER SUR UN
abricotier n'a pas pris...
C'est singulier, j'avais pourtant bien suivi la
méthode donnée par mon journal des
connaissances utiles!

My graft of a cherry slip on this apricot tree did not
take... Strange, I followed all the instructions in the
Manual of Useful Knowledge.

Del. 1394, second state
Pastorales
Pastoral Scenes
CHARIVARI, 22 June 1845

73

ET DIRE QUE C'EST AUJOURD'HUI LA ST. MÉDARD!
And to think that today is the 8th of June!

Del. 1401, second state
Pastorales
Pastoral Scenes
CHARIVARI, 10 July 1845

The scene is a simple country boardinghouse with pelting rain outside the window.
The boredom of the husband and wife flanked by two sullen children is extreme.
St. Médard was the French equivalent of the Anglo-Saxon St. Swithin. In both
countries, local tradition was that if rain fell on the saints' feast days, it would
continue for forty days.

74

COMMENT TROUVEZ-VOUS CE PETIT VIN-LÀ
How do you like this little wine?

Del. 1402, second state
Pastorales
Pastoral Scenes
CHARIVARI, 12 July 1845

PASTORALES.

Chez Aubert, Pl. de la Bourse.

Imp. d'Aubert &Cⁱᵉ.

— Et dire que c'est aujourd'hui la Sᵗ Médard !....

ALLONS BON!... VOILÀ LES GRAFIGNONS
qui viennent à six de Paris pour nous demander
à dîner sans façon et pas moyen de dire que
nous n'y sommes pas.

Good grief! Here come all six of the Grafignons
expecting to have dinner with us and we don't even
have the chance to say we are not here!

Del. 1405, second state
Pastorales
Pastoral Scenes
CHARIVARI, 14 August 1845

76

Not included in this exhibition.

77

AU SECOURS, AU SECOURS!... MON MARI
qui se bat contre un taureau!

Help, Help! My husband is fighting a bull!

Del. 1417, second state
Pastorales
Pastoral Scenes
CHARIVARI, 14 December 1845

The humor in the delightful set called *Pastorales* is often the depiction of the loss of
equilibrium suffered by urban folk when confronted by the simplest aspects of nature.
The landscape here suggests a feeling of Corot.

78

LE DERNIER JOUR DE LA RÉCEPTION DES TABLEAUX.
Saperlotte... Nous voici déjà arrivés et mon
tableau n'est pas fini!

The last day for accepting new pictures.
Good grief, here we are and my picture
not yet finished!

Del. 1472, second state
Actualités
Current Events
CHARIVARI, 20 February 1846

Scenes of artists, almost like self-portraits (which he seldom did), appear in Daumier's
work rather as interludes in the midst of political or social caricatures. It was as if he
drew himself up in the midst of *Actualités* or *Les Bons Bourgeois* to evaluate the state of
the Arts. Each scene is a document, and they are progressive throughout his years.

Chez Aubert & Cie Pl. de la Bourse, 29.

Imp. d'Aubert & Cie.

— Allons bon!... voila les Grafignons qui viennent à six de Paris pour nous demander à diner sans façon, et pas moyen de dire que nous n'y sommes pas!...

PASTORALES.

N° 50.

Au secours, au secours !... mon mari qui se bat contre un taureau !...

LE DERNIER JOUR DE LA RÉCEPTION DES TABLEAUX.

—Saperlotte! — nous voici déja arrivés, et mon tableau n'est pas fini... je suis fâché d'avoir pris mon commissionaire à la course, j'aurais mieux fait de le prendre à l'heure!....

LES BONS BOURGEOIS
The Middle Class

In a brilliant series, *Les Bons Bourgeois*, Daumier continued to chronicle from 1846 to 1849 unexpected moments in the lives of middle-class Parisians. A rare combination of observation and imagination produced seemingly effortless, unforgettable pictures. The fluidity of execution was in part made possible by the medium of lithography. Few artists have possessed the ability of Daumier to transcribe a fleeting movement onto stone with such authority. His drawing enhances life, so that even the unbelievable becomes natural.

79

QUAND LE JOURNAL EST TROP INTÉRESSANT
When the newspaper is too interesting

Del. 1488, third state
Les Bons Bourgeois
The Middle Class
CHARIVARI, 12 August 1846

80

POSITION RÉPUTÉE LA PLUS COMMODE POUR...
un portrait au daguerréotype
The most convenient way to pose for a Daguerreotype

Del. 1525, third state
Les Bons Bourgeois
The Middle Class
CHARIVARI, 27 July 1847

81

UNE POSITION DIFFICILE
An awkward position

Del. 1528, second state
Les Bons Bourgeois
The Middle Class
CHARIVARI, 1847, never published

82

RECHERCHE INFRUCTUEUSE DE LA
planète Leverrier
Unfruitful search for the planet Leverrier

Del. 1531, proof before letters
Les Bons Bourgeois
The Middle Class
CHARIVARI, 4 December 1846

LES BONS BOURGEOIS.

N.° 49.

Position réputée la plus commode pour avoir un joli portrait au Daguerréotype.

Chez Aubert & Cie Pl. de la Bourse, 29.

Imp. d'Aubert & Cie

Une position difficile.

83

UNE IDYLLE DANS LES BLÉS
An idyll in the wheatfield

Del. 1548, second state
Les Bons Bourgeois
The Middle Class
CHARIVARI, 6 September 1847

84

N'EST-CE PAS QUE MA MAISON...
est charmante d'ici?
Doesn't my house look charming from here?

Del. 1558, proof before letters
Les Bons Bourgeois
The Middle Class
1847, never published

LOCATAIRES ET PROPRIÉTAIRES
Tenants and Landlords

Under the July Monarchy, speculation by property owners developed new quarters to the northwest and west of Paris for luxury business, while the working men's districts were allowed to decay in sordid squalor. A rise in the city's population aggravated the need for housing for both middle and working classes. The nerves of both tenants and landlords were exacerbated. Daumier saw clearly both sides of troublesome urban problems.

85

BRIGAND DE PROPRIÉTAIRE
Rogue of a landlord

Del. 1605, first state, proof before letters
Locataires et Propriétaires
Tenants and Landlords
CHARIVARI, 26 May 1847

86

JE NE LOUE PAS AUX GENS QUI ONT DES ENFANTS!
I don't rent to families with children!

Del. 1607, second state
Locataries et Propriétaires
Tenants and Landlords
CHARIVARI, 24 June 1847

LES BONS BOURGEOIS.

N.º 72.

Une idylle dans les blés.

87

UN DÉMÉNAGEMENT FURTIF
Moving on the sly

Del. 1608, first state, proof before letters
Locataries et Propriétaires
Tenants and Landlords
CHARIVARI, 6 July 1847

88

UN LOCATAIRE QUI PAYE EXACTEMENT
son terme
The tenant who pays his rent promptly

Del. 1614, second state
Locataires et Propriétaires
Tenants and Landlords
CHARIVARI, 23 September 1847

89

L'OUBLI DE LA CONSIGNE
Having forgotten his instructions

Del. 1626, proof before letters
Locataries et Propriétaires (?)
Tenants and Landlords
1848 (?), never published

90

LE JARDIN SUR LA TERRASSE
The roof-garden

Del. 1627, proof before letters
Locataires et Propriétaires (?)
Tenants and Landlords
1848 (?), never published

LES BAIGNEUSES
The Bathers

The semi-nude bodies in the lithographs showing bathers are far from ideal, but, like the etchings of bathers by Rembrandt, these drawings from life have profound reality.

LOCATAIRES ET PROPRIÉTAIRES.

N.º 21.

Imp.Aubert & Cie

Chez Aubert, Pl. de la Bourse

Un locataire qui paye exactement son terme.

91

NAYADES DE LA SEINE
Naiads of the Seine

Del. 1629, second state
Les Baigneuses
The Bathers
CHARIVARI, 14 July 1847

92

ENTRE DEUX PLONGEONS
Between two dives

Del. 1632, second state
Les Baigneuses
The Bathers
CHARIVARI, 29 July 1847

TOUT CE QU'ON VOUDRA
Miscellany

The *Tout Ce Qu'on Voudra* series of twenty-nine lithographs made in the years 1847-1851 continues in the spirit *Les Bons Bourgeois*. Baudelaire, in a celebrated essay on humor, said that laughter sometimes contained an element of the satanic. The extraordinary point about Daumier's work is that his sense of wry raillery was a personal interpretation of individual acts under a universal umbrella. That is why he could be so comical. His invention flows easily without repetition in comment on the unforeseen accidents of life.

93

DIRE POURTANT QUE MES DAHLIAS CONTINUENT...
Somehow my dahlias continue to bloom

Del. 1652, second state
Tout Ce Qu'on Voudra (plate 6)
Miscellany
CHARIVARI, 1847, never published

94

INCONVÉNIENT D'UN PARAPLUIE
à ressorts trop compliqués
The inconvenience of an umbrella with a complex mechanism

Del. 1662, second state
Tout Ce Qu'on Voudra (plate 16)
Miscellany
CHARIVARI, 1847, never published

TOUT CE QU'ON VOUDRA.

— Dire pourtant que mes dalhias continuent encore cette année à être du ponceau le plus vif.... malgré tous mes soins, je ne pourrai donc jamais parvenir à leur donner la nuance **Boue de Paris !**...

TOUT CE QU'ON VOUDRA.

N.º 16.

Imp. Aubert & Cie.

Chez Aubert, Pl. de la Bourse.

Inconvénient d'un parapluie à ressorts trop compliqués.

95

C'EST T'Y À VOUS C'CHIEN LÀ?
Is that your dog?

Del. 1666, second state
Tout Ce Qu'on Voudra
Miscellany
CHARIVARI, 4 November 1847

96

OH!... ET TOI?... MOI AUSSI!
Oh!... And you?...Me too!

Del. 1671, proof before letters with written caption
Tout Ce Qu'on Voudra
Miscellany
CHARIVARI, 14 November 1847

97

Not included in this exhibition.

98

MOYEN D'ALLER CHERCHER LES BARBILLONS
dans leur propre domicile
How to find catfish in its own habitat

Del. 1678, second state
Tout Ce Qu'on Voudra
Miscellany
CHARIVARI, 1849

99

LE SPECTACLE EST UNE CHOSE BONNE
pour le peuple de paris. Il vient s'y délasser
le soir des fatigues de la journée.
*The theatre is good for the people of Paris. They come
here in the evening to relax from the fatigues of the day.*

Del. 1679, second state
Tout Ce Qu'on Voudra
Miscellany
CHARIVARI, 14 February 1849

Chez Aubert & C.ie Pl. de la Bourse 29

Imp. Aubert & C.ie

_ C'est t'y à vous c'hien là ?...

TOUT CE QU'ON VOUDRA

N° 52.

Moyen d'aller chercher les barbillons dans leur propre domicile

100

LA FEMME DOIT SUIVRE SON MARI
partout où il lui convient d'aller
élire son domicile.

*A wife must follow her husband wherever he chooses
to make his home.*

Del. 1692, second state
Tout Ce Qu'on Voudra
Miscellany
CHARIVARI, 31 May 1848

101

COMMENT PEUVENT-ILS TROUVER
amusant de rester...

How can they find it entertaining to stay...

Del. 1704, second state
Tout Ce Qu'on Voudra (plate 58)
Miscellany
CHARIVARI, 1850, never published

102

MANIÈRE POLIE DE METTRE... À LA PORTE
A polite way... to throw out

Del. 1723, second state
Scènes d'Ateliers
In the Studios
CHARIVARI, 21 June 1850

103

TOUT EST PERDU! FORS LA CAISSE...
All is lost! Save the cash box...

Del. 1744, second state
CHARIVARI, 7 March 1848

Following the February Revolution, Louis-Philippe arrives in England at the start
of his exile.

Chez Aubert Pl. de la Bourse

Imp. Aubert & Cie

La femme doit suivre son mari partout ou il lui convient d'aller élire son domicile.

(Code civil titre du mariage)

104

LE CONSTITUTIONNEL NAPOLÉONIEN
The Napoleonic "Constitutionnel"

Del. 1753, third state
Actualités
Current Events
CHARIVARI, 27 November 1848

Louis Désiré Véron was a Parisian doctor born in 1798. Before his death in 1883, he became both a politician and a publicist. In 1839 he bought *Le Constitutionnel*. He succeeded in making it a forceful newspaper that supported law and order, the government and the interests of the middle class.

105

VICTOR HUGO ET ÉMILE GIRARDIN
cherchent à élever le Prince Louis
Victor Hugo and Émile Girardin try to praise Prince Louis

Del. 1756, second state
CHARIVARI, 11 December 1848

In September 1848, Louis-Napoleon was elected to a seat in the Legislature. Here Victor Hugo, with averted face, and Émile Girardin are seen trying to promote the Prince to the highest office. Daumier doubted the wisdom of the poet's endorsement of the future Emperor.

106

LA TENTATION DU NOUVEAU ST. ANTOINE
(le docteur Véron)
The temptation of the new St. Anthony (Dr. Véron)

Del. 1912, second state
CHARIVARI, 24 October 1849

This is another of Daumier's comments on the activities of Dr. Véron. Dr. Véron did not like to be caricatured. He did, however, in 1854, write one of the few contemporary estimates of Daumier. "How living his characters are... With what power and fecundity he knows how to place them in scenes of passion and ridicule. He goes sometimes almost to the grotesque, but often he reveals with mastery the secret thoughts of the human heart."

LILLIPUTIENS ESSAYANT DE PROFITER DU
sommeil d'un nouveau Gulliver
*Lilliputians trying to take advantage of a new
sleeping Gulliver*

Del. 2010, unique state
Actualités
Current Events
CHARIVARI, 20-21 May 1850

In February 1848 Louis-Philippe went into exile. A new republic was formed with Louis-Bonaparte elected as President. Daumier viewed Napoleon III with less than enthusiasm. With his usual clairvoyance, he realized that a new Napoleonic era might be beneficial for France. Between the years 1848 and 1852, when the Second Empire was declared, he made a number of political lithographs. Here, the ministers of the Prince-President are seen immobilizing the supine figure of universal suffrage. The electorate was drastically reduced by the electoral law of 31 May 1850.

108

MAC-ADAM (sic) ET BINEAU AUX ENFERS
Par suite d'une punition terrible, mais méritée,
ils sont condamnés à repaver les Champs Élysées.
*MacAdam and Bineau in hell. Terrible but just punishment,
they are condemned to repave the Champs Élysées.*

Del. 2021, third state
Actualités
Current Events
CHARIVARI, 13 July 1850

John Loudon McAdam, a Scottish inventor (1756-1836), developed a system of road-making which came to be known as "macadamizing." An impervious cover was laid over subsoil kept dry by drainage. In *MacAdam and Bineau in Hell*, the suffering engineer, overseen by Pluto, is trying to repave the Champs Élysées by hand.

109

REAPPARITION DE LA JEUNESSE DORÉE EN 1851
Reappearance of the gilded youth in 1851

Del. 2121, second state
Actualités
Current Events
CHARIVARI, 30 June 1851

Two middle-aged republicans are seen convinced that they can recall their youthful sentiments. The upper part of the statue of the Republic of France is wisely hidden.

RATAPOIL

Ratapoil was one of Daumier's most successful imaginary characters who appeared in both a series of lithographs and as a sculpture (See cat. no. 235). Deriving his features from Louis-Napoleon himself, Ratapoil represented a sinister, unscrupulous figure committed to advancing the views of the new Prince-President.

110

AUX CHAMPS ÉLYSÉES, RATAPOIL...
Par suite d'une délibération philanthropique (sic)
du Comité du dix Décembre...à deux sous
les gourdins...à deux sous...
Result of the Tenth of December Committee's philanthropic
debate...two cents a club...two cents...

Del. 2126, second state
Actualités
Current Events
CHARIVARI, 12 July 1851

111

LES PRINCIPAUX PERSONNAGES DE LA
comédie qui se joue en ce moment
aux Champs Élysées
The main characters of the comedy now playing at the
Champs Élysées

Del. 2156, second state
Actualités
Current Events
CHARIVARI, 8 October 1851

112

RÊVANT QU'ELLE A GAGNÉ LE GROS
lingot d'or
Dreaming that she has won the jackpot

Del. 2162, second state
Actualités
Current Events
CHARIVARI, 27 October 1851

A château in the country, a small carriage with two footmen make up the dream of the aged harridan.

ACTUALITÉS.

Chez Aubert &Cie Pl. de la Bourse 29. Paris.

Imp. de Me Ve Aubert 5 r. de l'Abbaye à Paris

AUX CHAMPS-ÉLYSÉES.

Ratapoil — Par suite d'une délibération philantropique du Comité du **dix Décembre**
à deux sous les gourdins...... à deux sous!.......

Les Principaux Personnages de la Comédie qui se joue en ce moment aux Champs-Elysées

Chez Aubert & Cie Pl. de la Bourse, 29 Paris

Imp Ch. Trinocq Cour des Miracles, 9. Paris.

Rêvant qu'elle a gagné le gros lingot d'or.

CE QUI ADVIENDRAIT SI L'ON VOULAIT
tenter de nouveau le passage du Rubicon
What would happen if one attempted a new crossing
of the Rubicon

Del. 2169, second state
Actualités
Current Events
CHARIVARI, 22 November 1851

Near the Concorde Bridge three figures are trying to cross the Seine in an attempt to reach the Chamber of Deputies. The leader almost submerged is Louis Bonaparte, the future Napoleon III. The second is Ratapoil armed with his baton. A huge crowd on the quai watches their progress. The word Rubicon refers to the effort to restore universal suffrage which failed after the *coup d'état* which placed Napoleon III on the throne. The republicans were defeated.

114

L'AVOCAT: L'AFFAIRE MARCHE
Le plaideur: Vous me dites cela depuis quatre
ans. Si elle marche encore longtemps comme ça,
je finirai par n'avoir plus de bottes pour la suivre!
Lawyer: The case is moving along.
Client: You have been telling me that for four years. If it
continues at this pace, I will no longer have boots to follow it!

Del. 2185, second state
Les Avocats et les Plaideurs
Lawyers and Litigants
CHARIVARI, 12 November 1851

115

MOI J'AI POUR HABITUDE DE NE JAMAIS
rien donner au garçon, c'est encourager le célibat.
I never tip the waiter, it encourages celibacy.

Del. 2191, second state
Les Habitués des Cafés
Cafe Patrons
CHARIVARI, 17 December 1851

Chez Aubert & Cie Pl. de la Bourse, 29 Paris.   Imp.Ch Trinocq Cour des Miracles, 9. Paris.

L'avocat. —L'affaire marche, l'affaire marche!

Le plaideur.—Vous me dites cela depuis quatre ans; si elle marche encore longtemps comme ça, je finirai par n'avoir plus de bottes pour la suivre!..

LES HABITUÉS DES CAFÉS

Chez Pannier & Cⁱᵉ rue du Croissant, 16. Paris   Imp. Ch. Trinocq Cour des Miracles, 9. Paris.

— Moi, j'ai pour habitude de ne jamais rien donner au garçon, c'est encourager le célibat.

OUI, MADAME CHIFFLARD, LE GOUVERNEMENT
en a reçu la nouvelle ce matin par télégraphe
électrique, tous les raisins sont attaqués de la
maladie des pommes de terre.

*Yes, Madame Chifflard, the government received the news
this morning by telegram, all the grapes are infested with the
potato disease.*

Del. 2246, second state
Actualités
Current Events
CHARIVARI, 30 September 1851

To send a telegram in 1851 was still a novelty. The impact of the message on an astounded French housewife in Paris is shown by Daumier in this impressionistic street scene.

117

MADAME CHAPOTARD SE DISPOSANT
à faire ses confitures

Mrs. Chapotard preparing to make her jams

Del. 2314, second state
Scènes de la Vie de Province
Provincial Life
CHARIVARI, 7 July 1852

The smug Mrs. Chapotard is clearly not a lovable character. Her high-minded intention, however, is hardly a laughable matter. A greengrocer, burdened with sugar and wine, accepts one reality of provincial life. The making of homemade jam is no light affair.

118

L'OURS DU NORD, LE PLUS DÉSAGRÉABLE
de tous les ours connus

The northern bear, the most disagreeable bear known

Del. 2493, second state
Actualités
Current Events
CHARIVARI, 17-18 April 1854

The revolutions of 1848 that erupted in Italy, Germany, France, Austria and Poland were held in check in Russia by the stern measures of Czar Nicholas I. When Daumier turned his attention to the difficult Eastern questions that led to the Crimean War, he showed again a remarkable sense of historical values. Here the northern bear represents the Czar dominating the Russian people.

SCENES DE LA VIE DE PROVINCE

Maison Martinet, r. Vivienne 41 et 11 r. du Coq. Paris.

Imp. Ch. Trinocq Cour des Miracles, 9. Paris.

Madame Chapotard se disposant à faire ses confitures.

ACTUALITÉS.

L'Ours du nord, le plus désagréable de tous les ours connus .

G

LE 14 JUIN
Dieu soit loue...le 13 Juin est passé...
et nous sommes encore vivants!

June 14
Thank God, the 13th has come and gone...and we are
still alive!

Del. 2657, second state
Les Bons Parisiens
Good Old Parisians
CHARIVARI, 15 June 1857

120

EXPOSITION EN PLEIN VENT DES
provinciaux venus à Paris pour voir
le palais de l'Industrie

Tourists from the provinces blown in to see the
industrial exhibition

Del. 2694, second state
L'Exposition Universelle
The World's Fair
CHARIVARI, 16-17 August 1855

The World's Fair of 1855 drew thousands of people from the provinces. The inconveniences of traveling, the lack of shelter in the city and the wonders of the great industrial exhibition were all subjects for Daumier's crayon.

121

ASPECT DES BOULEVARDS PENDANT
la foire aux bibelots

Appearance of the boulevards during the curio fair

Del. 2736, second state
Actualités
Current Events
CHARIVARI, 7 January 1856

122

ÉMIGRATION

Emigration

Del. 2737, second state
Actualités
Current Events
CHARIVARI, 12 January 1856

In 1856 Daumier drew a little known lithograph of emigrating dogs. Tails down, eyes fixed on some unknown destination, they move as a group. There is a kinship in intensity between their haunting movement and the bas-relief of the same title. The human drama of the famous sculpture finds a striking parallel with the animals who have become anthropomorphic figures.

LE 14 JUIN.

_ Dieu soit loué,.....le 13 juin est passé.....et nous sommes encore vivants!...

Exposition en plein vent des provinciaux venus à Paris pour voir le Palais de l'industrie.

122 (Del. 2737)

Émigration.

123

ET DIRE QU'ON NOUS INTERDIT D'ENTRER
là dedans pour faire aussi nos petites affaires...
And to think we are forbidden to go in there and take care of our own business...

Del. 2756, second state
Les Boursicotières
Dabbling in the Stock Market
CHARIVARI, 2 October 1856

124

PRENEZ-MOI ÇA DE CONFIANCE,
ça sera tendre comme du poulet
Trust me, it will be tender as chicken

Del. 2780, second state
Les Hippophages
The Horsemeat Fanciers
CHARIVARI, 3 March 1856

In a series of ten lithographs (1856-1858), Daumier pictured the strange behavior of people inclined to eat horsemeat. This is a mordant series. A skeletal horse barely able to move is the object of bargaining by horsemeat dealers who are scarcely more attractive than their prey.

125

MÔSSIEU LE CONCIERGE
His Excellency, the doorkeeper

Del. 2813, second state
Croquis Parisiens
Parisian Sketches
CHARIVARI, 25 November 1856

126

UN RAPPEL DE CHANTEUSE...
scène de haute comédie
Encore for the singer...scene of high comedy

Del. 2905, third state
Croquis Dramatiques
Stage Sketches
CHARIVARI, 9 January 1857

Prenez moi ça de confiance, ça sera tendre comme du poulet !.....

Im.ᵉ Martinet, 146, r Rivoli, et et 41, p.Vivienne.

Lith Destouches, 28, r. Paradis P.ˢⁿ Paris

Môssieu le concierge.

Un rappel de chanteuse ;.....scéne de haute comédie.

127

LA MÈRE DE L'AMOUR
(ne pas confondre avec Vénus)
The mother of love (not to be confused with Venus)

Del. 2906, second state
Croquis Dramatiques
Stage Sketches
CHARIVARI, 20 January 1857

In these two vignettes of scenes at the theater, it is the play of light on the stage that is important. The lithographs suggest comparison with similar exercises by Degas.

128

DANGER DE PORTER DES JUPONS-BALLONS
à l'époque des coups de vent de l'équinoxe
The danger of wearing hoop skirts at the time of the equinox

Del. 2917, second state
La Crinolomanie
Crinolomania
CHARIVARI, 3 April 1857

From the mid-fifties, Daumier's work shows a growth, a largeness of design and a freedom in drawing that is easy to recognize now as the inevitable development of genius. His major themes during that period were *En Chemin de Fer* (Railroads), *Croquis Dramatiques* (Dramatic Sketches), *Croquis pris à l'Exposition* (Exhibition Sketches), and *Croquis pris au Salon* (Sketches made at the Salon).

129

ASPECT QUE COMMENCENT DÉJÀ À AVOIR
chaque soir les rues de Paris
Paris streets are beginning to look like this every night

Del. 2931, second state
La Comète de 1857
The Comet of 1857
CHARIVARI, 21 March 1857

Ten prints illustrating the effect of the "Comet of 1857" on Parisians were published in the *Charivari* in 1857.

130

ASPECT DU SALON LE JOUR DE L'OUVERTURE -
rien que de vrais connaisseurs (sic),
total soixante mille personnes
*The Salon on opening day - only the true connoisseurs,
sixty thousand souls in all*

Del. 2959, second state
Le Salon de 1857
The Salon of 1857
CHARIVARI, 22 June 1857

Maison Martinet 172 y Rivoli et 41 y Vivienne

Lith Destouches 28 y Paradis P^{re} Paris.

Danger de porter des jupons-ballons à l'époque des coups de vent de l'équinoxe.

Aspect du salon le jour de l'ouverture, _ rien que de vrais connaisseurs, total soixante mille personnes.

131

COMMENT, C'EST DANS CETTE CAVE QUE
sont les sculptures...je n'irai pas les voir,
j'ai peur des rats.
What, the sculptures are in this cellar?
Never mind seeing them, I am afraid of rats.

Del. 2960, second state
Le Salon de 1857
The Salon of 1857
CHARIVARI, 2 July 1857

132

J'AIMERAIS AUTANT VOIR UN OURAGAN
se promener dans mon jardin qu'une
de ces satanées crinolines!...
I would rather see a hurricane walking around my garden
than these darned crinolines!...

Del. 2972, second state
Actualités
Current Events
CHARIVARI, 9 September 1857

The crinoline, as a style, was suitable for the Court of the Empress, when painted by
Winterhalter, or for the demi-mondaines as drawn by Guys. Daumier's picture of the
absurdity of such clothing for an ordinary woman walking about the routine paths of
daily life is more than devastating.

133

INCONVÉNIENT DES JUPONS À RESSORT
en acier, quand ce ressort vient à se casser
The trouble with steel reinforced petticoats, when the
spring breaks

Del. 2976, second state
Croquis Parisiens
Parisian Sketches
CHARIVARI, 18 August 1857

134

SOUVENIR DU GRAND FESTIVAL
des Orphéonistes
Recollection of the Grand Festival of the Choral Society

Del. 3131, second state
Actualités
Current Events
CHARIVARI, 28 March 1859

ACTUALITES. 431.

m^{on} Martinet, 172, r Rivoli et 41, r Vivienne.
Lith. Destouches, 28 r. Paradis P^{se}. Paris.

_ J'aimerais autant voir un ouragan se promener dans mon jardin qu'une de ces satanées crinolines !...

maison Martinet , 172 r Rivoli et 41 r Vivienne   Lith Destouches 28 r Paradis P.se Paris .

Inconvénient des jupons à ressort en acier, quand ce ressort vient à se casser.

135

ASPECT DE LA SALLE
Plan, coupe, hauteur et élévation des chefs
d'orchestre. Alliance de la télégraphie
et de la musique.
Overview of the hall
Plan, cross section, elevation and side view of the
conductors. Alliance of music and telegraphy.

Del. 3132, unique state
Souvenir du Grand Festival des Orphéonistes
Recollections of the Grand Festival of the Choral Society
CHARIVARI, 2 April 1859

136

LE PEINTRE QUI A EU UN TABLEAU REFUSÉ
The artist whose painting has been rejected

Le Peintre:	Mossieur, ne trouvez-vous pas ce tableau horrible...et comprenez-vous que le jury ait accepté une pareille croûte?
Le Monsieur:	Mais je trouve que la personne qui l'a fait a beaucoup de talent!... c'est charmant!
Le Peintre:	Je vois que mossieu est un ami du peintre, mossieu aura même, sans doute, posé pour ce tableau.
The Artist:	*Sir, don't you find this a horrible picture...do you understand how the jury could have accepted such a dog?*
The Gentleman:	*But I think the person who painted it has lots of talent! It's charming!*
The Artist:	*I see, Sir, that you are a friend of the painter...perhaps you even posed for the picture.*

Del. 3141, second state
Exposition de 1859
Exhibition of 1859
CHARIVARI, 23 April 1859

Daumier spent the summer of 1853 at Valmondois. While there, he renewed his friendships with the painters of the Barbizon School: Corot, Rousseau and Millet. All were struggling for acceptance in the salons. The indiscriminating public, however, flocked to the exhibitions. Taine wrote, "How does one sell six or seven miles of painting from the salon?" It was answered by Daumier in a set of nine lithographs on The Exhibition of 1859. In each picture Daumier drew facial expressions of the unenlightened groping for understanding before banal pictures, while gifted artists are portrayed as enraged, discouraged or mute.

1

mᵐ Martinet 172. r. Rivoli et 41, r. Vivienne

Lith.Destouches 28. r.Paradis P¹ᵉ Paris.

Aspect de la salle. _ Plan, coupe, hauteur et élévation des chefs d'orchestre _ *Alliance de la télégraphie et de la musique*.

137

MON AMI...LÂCHE-LUI TA CANNE...
il pourrait t'entraîner dans la mer!
My friend, let go of the cane...it could drag you into the sea!

Del. 3209, second state
Aux Bains de Mer
At the Seashore
CHARIVARI, 28 September 1859

The struggle between a ferocious lobster and a terrified vacationer is the most successful lithograph in a series of six plates called *Aux Bains de Mer* (At the Seashore). The calm sea in the background drawn with few lines heightens the drama between the two unlikely protagonists in the foreground.

SOUVENIRS D'ARTISTES
Artists' Recollections

Daumier left *Charivari* in February of 1860. It is not entirely clear whether he was dismissed or withdrew of his own accord to devote his time to painting. In any case, his friends were concerned both about his poor health and his financial situation. One of Daumier's friends, Étienne Carjat, a journalist-photographer-artist, founded, in 1861, an illustrated journal called *Le Boulevard*. Banville and Baudelaire were literary contributors to it. Daumier supplied ten lithographic masterpieces for the new publication, two of which were *Madeleine-Bastille* and the following entry, *Le Dimanche au Jardin des Plantes* (Sunday in the Botanical Gardens). In this series Daumier is to be seen at the height of his graphic powers. The new monumentality of design appears to flow across these white pages with seemingly effortless grace. All ten subjects, with one additional plate *L'Âne et les Deux Voleurs* (The Donkey and the Two Thieves), were re-issued under the title *Souvenirs d'Artistes* by the printer Bertaut.

138

MADELEINE-BASTILLE. UN ZESTE,
un rien...et l'omnibus se trouve complet.
A trifle...the bus is full.

Del. 3243, second state, laid china paper
Souvenirs d'Artistes
Artists' Recollections
LE BOULEVARD, 16 March 1862

The words "Madeleine-Bastille" signify one of the bus routes through Paris.

imp. Martinet, 172, r. Rivoli et 41, r. Vivienne . Lith Destouches, 28, r. Paradis Pte Paris .

— Mon ami ..., lâche lui ta canne .....il pourrait t'entraîner dans la mer !......

MADELEINE – BASTILLE

Un zeste, un rien.... et l'omnibus se trouve complet.

LE DIMANCHE AU JARDIN DES PLANTES
Sunday in the botanical gardens

Del. 3244, second state, laid china paper
Souvenirs d'Artistes
Artists' Recollections
LE BOULEVARD, 23 March 1862

The Botanical Gardens, a green oasis in the heart of Paris, were established by
Guy de la Brosse in 1635 in the reign of Louis XIII. It was designed originally as a
garden of medicinal plants. Over the centuries, zoological, mineral and a wide variety
of botanical rarities were added to the collection. During the Revolution, when much
of the national heritage in churches, chateaux and other public buildings was ravaged,
the Botanical Gardens were not only spared but greatly augmented. In the nineteenth
century they became a favorite place not only for children and their nurses but for
artists. Delacroix went there often to draw the lions in their abominable cages and
Daumier to observe the populace ambling along the winding paths. This moving, very
great lithograph of Daumier's illustrates vividly that the garden was a great magnet to
lessen the boredom of Sunday afternoon in the city.

LE NOUVEAU PARIS
Comme c'est heureux pour les gens pressés,
qu'on ait élargi les voies de communication!!!
The New Paris
How fortunate for people in a great hurry that the streets have been widened!!!

Del. 3245, second state
Souvenirs d'Artistes
Artists' Recollections
LE BOULEVARD, 6 April 1862

Baron Georges Eugène Haussmann (1809-1891) was a French civil servant whose
name is associated with the rebuilding of Paris. He was engaged as Prefect by the
Emperor Louis-Napoleon III to modernize the ancient city. During his tenure of office
the Bois de Boulogne was extensively improved, the Opera started, new bridges
constructed, and most important, new boulevards were cut across narrow streets to
accommodate the ever increasing traffic. The astonished population of the city was
greatly inconvenienced during fifteen years of "Haussmannization."

Le Dimanche au Jardin des Plantes.

LE NOUVEAU PARIS.

Imp. Bertauts Paris.

Comme c'est heureux pour les gens pressés qu'on ait élargi les voies de communication!!!

141

À TRAVERS LES ATELIERS
Fichtre!...Épatant!...Sapristi...Superbe...ça parle!...

In the Studios
Wow!...Amazing!...Gosh!...Superb!...it sings!...

Del. 3246, second state
Souvenirs d'Artistes
Artists' Recollections
LE BOULEVARD, 20 April 1862

Here six connoisseurs are seen examining a painting on an easel. Daumier made at least six drawings on the theme of visitors to the studio of a painter. The large watercolor in the Walters Art Gallery is well known. A small sketch in pencil over crayon in the same gallery is more closely related to the lithograph.

142

À LA VARENNE-ST. MAUR
La voilà...ma maison de campagne

At La Varenne-St. Maur
Here it is...my country house

Del. 3247, second state
Souvenirs d'Artistes
Artists' Recollections
LE BOULEVARD, 11 May 1862

This impression is one of the few known proofs pulled on thin India paper.

143

NADAR ÉLEVANT LA PHOTOGRAPHIE
à la hauteur de l'art
Nadar elevating photography to the height of art

Del. 3248, first state, laid china paper
Souvenirs d'Artistes
Artists' Recollections
LE BOULEVARD, 25 May 1862

In 1856 Félix Tournachon, better known as Nadar, made a celebrated ascent in a balloon over Paris. His extraordinary aerial photographs of the city marked a new chapter in the history of art.

A TRAVERS LES ATELIERS

Imp. Bertauts, Paris

Fichtre!... Epatant!... Sapristi!... Superbe!... ça parle!...

A la Varenne St Maur.

La Voilà!.. ma maison de Campagne!...

NADAR élevant la Photographie à la hauteur de l'Art

PAYSAGISTES AU TRAVAIL

Artists at work

Del. 3251, second state, laid china paper
Souvenirs d'Artistes
Artists' Recollections
LE BOULEVARD, 17 August 1862

The lyrical beauty of this landscape scene is unsurpassed in all of Daumier's lithographic work. Distant mountains enclose a small plain where the sunlight is caught magically falling on the two open parasols.

EN CHEMIN DE FER...UN VOISIN AGRÉABLE

On the train...A pleasant companion

Del. 3252, third state, laid china paper
Souvenirs d'Artistes
Artists' Recollections
LE BOULEVARD, 21 September 1862

L'ÂNE ET LES DEUX VOLEURS

The ass and the two thieves

Del. 3253, third state
Souvenirs d'Artistes
Artists' Recollections
LE BOULEVARD, 1862, never published

One aspect of Daumier's graphic genius has been too little explored — illustrator of the classics. He had a predilection for the works of La Fontaine, Cervantes and Molière. He illustrated the themes inspired by these authors in a highly personal manner. Here the fable of two thieves and a donkey transcends the usual idiom of illustration.

LA MUSE DE LA BRASSERIE

The muse of the tavern

Del. 3260, second state
À La Brasserie
At the Tavern
CHARIVARI, 21 January 1864

The charming figure of a woman standing alone is seen silhouetted against the men's heads in the crowded café. A similar composition was explored later by Édouard Manet in two of his most successful prints.

Paysagistes au travail...

_ En Chemin de Fer _ Un Voisin agréable.

Souvenirs d'Artistes.

H.Daumier, pinx. et lith.

Imp Bertauts, r.Cadet, 11, Paris.

L'Ane et les deux voleurs

A LA BRASSERIE

4.

La Muse de la Brasserie

CROQUIS PRIS AU THÉÂTRE
Theater Sketches

The following two lithographs are from a series of eight pieces illustrating scenes in the theater which were published irregularly in *Charivari* from February 1864 to June 1865.

148

LES SPECTATEURS DE L'ORCHESTRE
Il y a de jolies jambes...tous satisfaits.

Front row spectators
There are some pretty legs...everyone pleased.

Del. 3262, third state
Croquis Pris au Théâtre
Theater Sketches
CHARIVARI, 9 April 1864

149

MONSIEUR COLIMARD SI VOUS CONTINUEZ
à lorgner les danseuses d'une façon aussi
inconvenante je vous ramène à la maison
avant la fin du spectacle.

Mr. Colimard, if you continue to ogle the dancers in such
an improper way, I will take you back home before the end
of the performance.

Del. 3266, second state
Croquis Pris au Théâtre
Theater Sketches
CHARIVARI, 4 May 1864

150

LE DÉPART DE L'HIVER
Comment, vous songez déjà à nous quitter?...
Vous notre meilleur allié!...

The departure of winter
What, you want to leave so soon?...You, our strongest ally!...

Del. 3271, second state
Actualités
Current Events
CHARIVARI, 9 March 1864

In 1863 Daumier returned to work for *Charivari*. Here two Russian generals are pictured before a sign indicating the road to Poland. To the right a large figure personifying winter is their ally.

CROQUIS PRIS AU THÉATRE PAR DAUMIER

Mon Martinet, 172 r. Rivoli et 41 r. Vivienne

Lith Destouches, 28 r Paradis Pre

LES SPECTATEURS DE L'ORCHESTRE
Il y a de jolies jambes ... tous satisfaits !

CROQUIS PRIS AU THÉÂTRE par DAUMIER.   4

— Monsieur Colimard si vous continuez à lorgner les danseuses d'une façon aussi inconvenante je vous ramène à la maison avant la fin du spectacle.

LE DEPART DE L'HIVER

— Comment, vous songez déja à nous quitter ? . . . . vous notre meilleur allié ! . . .

151

EN CHEMIN DE FER. NOUS APPROCHONS
de ce grand tunnel où depuis le commencement
du mois il y a déjà eu trois accidents.
We are approaching the long tunnel where there have already
been three accidents this month.

Del. 3273, second state
Les Moments Difficiles de la Vie
Life's Difficult Moments
CHARIVARI, 16 March 1864

152

POUR LA SEPTIÈME FOIS, VOULEZ-VOUS
me rendre ma place?
-Sinon quoi.
-Sinon je serai obligé de m'en aller, ce qui me
contrarierai beaucoup!
-For the seventh time, will you move from my seat?
-Otherwise what.
-Otherwise I will have to go away, which will be very
repugnant to me!

Del. 3274, third state
Les Moments Difficiles de la Vie
Life's Difficult Moments
CHARIVARI, 23 March 1864

153

UN AMATEUR DIFFICILE
Je ne suis pas content du Salon cette année...
voilà du jambon qui laisse beaucoup à désirer...
au point de vue de la couleur.
A difficult patron of the arts.
I am unhappy with the Salon this year...this ham leaves
much to be desired...the color, I mean.

Del. 3291, second state
Croquis Pris à l'Exposition
Exhibition Images
CHARIVARI, 17 June 1864

The frustrated gallery visitor seated in the refreshment room adjoining the exhibition
finds the mediocrity of his ham equivalent to that of the paintings.

EN CHEMIN DE FER

— Nous approchons de ce grand Tunnel ou depuis le commencement du mois il y a déja eu trois accidents !....

M. PRUD'HOMME - VIVE LES WAGONS
de troisième classe. On peut y être
asphyxié mais jamais assassiné.
Mr. Prud'homme: Hurrah for third class cars. One can be
asphyxiated, but never assassinated.

Del. 3299, third state
En Chemin de Fer
The Railroads
CHARIVARI, 30 August 1864

Joseph Prud'homme, a man of substance with strongly held views and a specialist
in commonplace utterances, was a fictional person created by Henri Monnier,
the caricaturist, actor and playwright. After Monnier wrote and acted the farce,
The Improvised Family, Prud'homme became common property. His punch-like
profile, spectacled eyes and awkward bulging stomach were easily recognized by all.
Daumier has pictured him here complacently occupying more than his share of room
in a third class railroad carriage.

EH! BIEN, CROIS-TU QUE JE SERAI EMBARRASSÉ
pour vendre avantageusement cette étude là?
-Non...seulement il faut tomber sur
quelqu'un qui aime bien les peupliers.
-Do you think I'll have any trouble getting a good price for this study?
-No...but you'll have to find someone who's crazy about poplars.

Del. 3415, second state
Les Artistes
Artists
CHARIVARI, 19 January 1865

UN INVITÉ À UN DÎNER D'HIPPOPHAGES
Vous offrirai-je encore un peu?
C'est excellent, n'est-ce pas?
A guest at a dinner for horsemeat fanciers
Would you like a bit more?...Excellent, isn't it?

Del. 3424, second state
Actualités
Current Events
CHARIVARI, 24 March 1865

In the 1850s the strange cult that considered horsemeat a delicacy spread throughout
France. Clubs for gourmands of horsemeat sprang up from Toulouse to Paris.
Banquets were held by the members of these grotesque clubs. The tables were laden
with horseshoes, nails and bones. The folly of such pretentious nonsense did not
escape Daumier's attention. The artist's mild satire of an earlier (1856-1858) series of
ten plates on hippophagists here has turned mordant. The drawing of the skeletal
head of the horse on a platter surrounded by parsley is devastating.

Mon Martinet, 172, r. Rivoli et 41, r. Vivienne

Lith Destouches, 28, r. Paradis

M. PRUD'HOMME — Vive les wagons de troisième classe on peut y être asphyxié mais jamais assassiné.

M. Martinet, 172, r. Rivoli et 41, r. Vivienne.   Lith Destouches 28, r. Paradis P^{se}

_Eh! bien crois.tu que je serai embarassé pour vendre avantageusement cette étude là.

_Non... seulement il faut tomber sur quelqu'un qui aime bien les peupliers.

UN INVITÉ A UN DINER D'HIPPOPHAGES.

_ Vous offrirai _je encore un peu ?..... c'est excellent n'est ce pas !....

158 (Del. 3458)

Le roi des Potirons recevant les hommages de ses sujets.

157

NOUVELLE CHARCUTERIE PARISIENNE —
nouveaux pieds à la Ste. Ménehould inventés
par les hippophages.
New Parisian delicacy — feet à la St. Ménehould devised by
the Hippophagian society.

Del. 3437, second state
Croquis du Jour
Daily Sketches
CHARIVARI, 22 April 1865

Saint Ménehould was one of seven daughters of Count Sigmarus, a sixth century
nobleman of Perthois. All seven were venerated in different parts of Champagne. The
delicate meat is to be cooked according to the traditions followed in that province.

158

LE ROI DES POTIRONS RECEVANT
les hommages de ses sujets
The king of pumpkins receiving the homage of his subjects

Del. 3458, second state
Croquis d'Automne
Autumn Sketches
CHARIVARI, 25 September 1865

159

EUX AU MOINS NE REVIENNENT PAS BREDOUILLES
mais ils ne diront à personnes (sic) qu'ils
ont eu la chance de rencontrer des braconniers.
These fellows, at least, didn't come back empty-handed, but
they won't mention to a soul their luck in meeting poachers.

Del. 3467, second state
Croquis de Chasse
The Hunt
CHARIVARI, n.d. 1865

Two aristocratic gentlemen are pictured returning from the hunt with their trophies.
The hound dogs and the coachman appear ashamed of the day's work. Daumier, who
often sketched the pleasures of the hunt, in this rare lithograph offers a cynical
portrayal of the seedy side of the sport.

CROQUIS DE CHASSE par DAUMIER

Mᵒⁿ Martinet, Paris

lith. Destouches, 28, r. Paradis Pˢᵉ

_ Eux au moins ne reviennent pas BREDOUILLES mais ils ne diront a personnes qu'ils ont eu la chance de rencontrer des braconniers .et de leur acheter tout leur gibier.

160

CHANGEANT SON CHEVAL BORGNE POUR UN AVEUGLE
Changing his one-eyed horse for a blind one

Del. 3512, second state
Actualités
Current Events
CHARIVARI, 30 July 1866

In this political cartoon the reference is made to elections in England. The one-eyed horse on the left represènts the Whig party. John Bull is now seated on a blind horse — the Tory ministry.

161

ÉQUILIBRE EUROPÉEN
European balancing act

Del. 3566, second state
CHARIVARI, 3 April 1867

Daumier's cartoons from 1860 to 1871 show a comprehension of history that goes beyond national preoccupations. In many of these somber pictures there is a growing sense of foreboding, as the artist foresaw the inevitability of the Franco-Prussian war. *Équilibre européen* is possibly the most memorable of all these late images. A terrified woman symbolizing Europe is seen desperately trying to balance herself on a fusing bomb. The introduction of a new political rhetoric projects this picture into the twentieth century world of political cartoons. It is only a short step from this lithograph to the work of Herblock.

162

LE CHARIVARI. OBLIGÉ DE REFAIRE
une novelle vue...
The Charivari. Forced to rearrange the landscape...

Del. 3610, second state
CHARIVARI, 26 November 1867

Here Daumier has re-drawn the logo of *Charivari*. The jaunty mocker of the mid-century is presented transformed into a mature anxious man. He is reporting on his tablet the military maneuvers on the parade grounds near the Invalides.

A de Vresse rue Rivoli 55

Lith Destouches rue Paradis P^{re} 28

Equilibre Européen.

Le Charivari. Obligé de refaire prochainement une nouvelle vue de l'emplacement où s'élevait le temple de la Paix.

163

UN PEU AGÉE POUR JOUER AU COLOSSE
de Rhodes

A bit old to play "Colossus of Rhodes"

Del. 3612, second state
Actualités
Current Events
CHARIVARI, 10 December 1867

It is small wonder that Daumier personified diplomacy as a frail old lady dependent on the support of a cane. The artist had followed attentively the course of diplomacy in Europe from the time of Talleyrand for more than thirty years. As the aged woman edges forward hesitating between Italy and the Orient, the yawning abyss in the center underscores the punishment of one misstep.

164

UN PROCÉDÉ POUR QU'IL MARCHE
sans avancer

A system for walking without making headway

Del. 3645, third state
Actualités
Current Events
CHARIVARI, 19 June 1868

In the first state Daumier had drawn the figure of a Jesuit with a whip in his hand. The figure was effaced in later impressions.

165

VOUS CROYEZ PEUT-ÊTRE QUE C'EST UN SPECTATEUR...
Eh bien pas même!...C'est le directeur!!

You may think this is a spectator...Well, hardly!...it's the director!!

Del. 3653, second state
Actualités
Current Events
CHARIVARI, 29 July 1868

Un peu agée pour jouer au colosse de Rhodes

Vous croyez peut être que c'est un spectateur........ eh bien pas même !.......c'est le directeur !!!

166

MONSIEUR L'ACADÉMICIEN, JE SUIS CANDIDAT
au fauteuil de M. Viennet.

Professor, I am a candidate for Mr. Viennet's chair.

Del. 3654, second state
Actualités
Current Events
CHARIVARI, 31 July 1868

Daumier's modesty was proverbial. In 1870 he refused to accept the Cross of the Legion of Honor. When asked by Courbet his reason, Daumier replied, "I did what I thought I ought to do. I am content, and it is no concern of the public." It is understandable why he would depict with scorn two academicians reaching for honors and fame.

167

-FAISONS SEMBLANT DE DORMIR
car il serait capable de me développer son amendement sur le dernier projet de loi.
-Il faut qu'il croie que je dorme, sans quoi il prendrait la parole sur le procès verbal de la dernière séance.

-I'll pretend to be asleep, otherwise he's likely to expound on his plans for amending the latest bill.
-I must convince him that I am asleep or he will go on and on about the proceedings of the last session.

Del. 3661, third state
Actualités
Current Events
CHARIVARI, 9 September 1868

168

AU CAMP DE CHALONS
The camp at Chalons

Del. 3729, second state
Actualités
Current Events
CHARIVARI, 19 August 1869

The man standing under the umbrella is the familiar character, Mr. Prud'homme. His son points to the soldiers marching at the military camp of Chalons. They exercise in the rain, in preparation for battle.

ACTUALITÉS.

A. de Vresse, r, Rivoli, 55.

Lith. Destouches, r. Paradis P^{te} 28.

— Faisons semblant de dormir car il serait capable de me développer son amendement sur le dernier projet de loi. — Il faut qu'il croie que je dorme, sans quoi il prendrait la parole sur le procès verbal de la dernière séance.

9 sept. 1868

AU CAMP DE CHALONS

— Papa, pourquoi faire sortir ces soldats par ce temps de pluie.

— Mon ami c'est pour leur apprendre à aller au feu.

G
L

UN CAUCHEMAR DE M. DE BISMARK.

— Merci !...

GL

169

UN CAUCHEMAR DE M. BISMARK (sic)

Bismarck's nightmare

Del. 3802, second state
CHARIVARI, 22 August 1870

Under a tent the German Chancellor is represented asleep in an armchair. Death with his grim scythe seizes the arm of Bismarck to awaken him and point out his accomplishments: a field of corpses.

170

CEUX QUI VONT MOURIR TE SALUENT!

We who are about to die salute you!

Del. 3804, second state
Actualités
Current Events
CHARIVARI, 2 September 1870

171

L'EMPIRE C'EST LA PAIX

The Empire means peace

Del. 3814, third state
Actualités
Current Events
CHARIVARI, 19 October 1870

This lithograph appeared in an album containing pictures of the siege of Paris during the Franco-Prussian War. It is a tragic allegory. Louis-Napoleon's dreams of an empire have ended in desolation.

L'EMPIRE C'EST LA PAIX.

PAUVRE FRANCE!... LE TRONC EST FOUDROYÉ, MAIS LES RACINES TIENNENT BON!

172

PAUVRE FRANCE...LE TRONC EST FOUDROYÉ
mais les racines tiennent bon.
Poor France...The trunk was struck by lightning, but the roots hold fast.

Del. 3843, third state
Actualités
Current Events
CHARIVARI, 1 February 1871

A large oak tree badly battered by lightning is revealed in the clearing air to have tenacious roots. This is another powerful piece of propaganda made by Daumier during the Franco-Prussian War.

173

LA FUSION
Bien entendu que les malins laissent croire
à la porte que le phénomène est vivant.
Fusion
Of course, mischievous people lead one to believe
that the monster is still alive.

Del. 3913, first state
CHARIVARI, 16 March 1872

A glass jar contains a monstrous double-headed fetus. In 1872 Daumier was concerned with the struggles to establish the Third Republic. The hopes of both the Legitimists and the Orléanists were still alive. In this lithograph Daumier pictures both claimants as already embalmed.

174

EN ESPAGNE - CHARITÉ CHRÉTIENNE
In Spain - Christian charity

Del. 3929, second state
CHARIVARI, 29 May 1872

Daumier in his graphic work was strongly anticlerical. This rare sardonic statement represents an armed Jesuit in the Pyrenées Mountains.

EN ESPAGNE. — CHARITÉ CHRÉTIENNE.

100

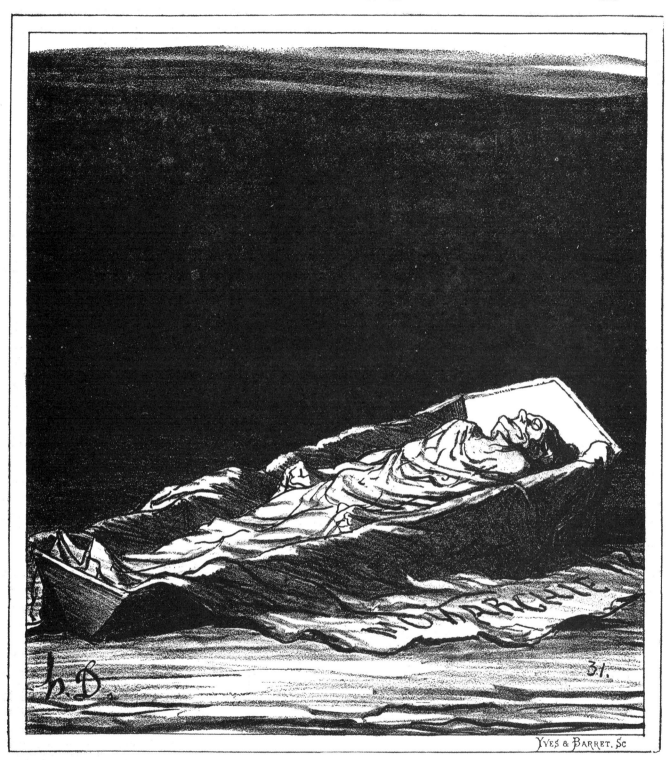

Et pendant ce temps-là ils continuent à affirmer qu'elle ne s'est jamais mieux portée !

ET PENDANT CE TEMPS-LÀ ILS CONTINUENT
à affirmer qu'elle ne s'est jamais mieux portée!
They still maintain she never felt better!

Del. 3937, second state
Actualités
Current Events
CHARIVARI, 24 September 1872

This picture is Daumier's last great political cartoon. A stark cadaver wrapped in a shroud lies in an open coffin. Unrelieved blackness fills three-quarters of the composition. The word spelled out on the winding sheet signifies the death of the monarchy. Even Daumier's initials in the lower left seem to emphasize the end of a long era.

JE N'AI JAMAIS TANT RI QU'À L'ENTERREMENT
de la fille à Bourdin
I have never laughed so hard as I did at the funeral of Bourdin's girl.

Del. 3250, third state
LE BOULEVARD, 3 August 1862

—Je n'a. jamais tant ri qu'a l'enterrement de la fille à Bourdin......

(Henry Monnier)

176b

Lithographic stone
Height: 26.7 cm; width: 32.0 cm; depth: 5.1 cm

CHARBON DE BOIS DE L'ENTREPÔT D'IVRY
The cook and the charcoal man

Del. (Appendix) 27
Two color lithograph (122.0 x 90.2 cm)
ca. 1872

Charles Desouches, the founder and director of the charcoal warehouse of Ivry, was a sculptor and a friend of Daumier's. Desouches lived near Daumier from 1865 to 1872 on the Île St. Louis. Then he moved to 30 Rue Geoffroy-Lasnier, the address which appears at the bottom of the poster. The warehouse for the charcoal was located in the suburb of Ivry. The charcoal merchant often entertained the artist. On one such occasion he asked the artist to make a poster for his firm to replace an earlier design made by Emile Bayard about 1855. Daumier drew his poster with pen and ink on stone, probably in 1872.

There are only eleven known impressions of Daumier's famous design, three of which are now in the Museum of Fine Arts, Boston. This impression was printed by L. Péquerau, 4 Rue et Place Louvois. Delteil illustrated it without the border in 1929, when it was in the possession of Le Garrec, grandson of Philipon. It was already in America in 1934, when Anna C. Hoyt wrote her important article (1945) on the confusing bibliographical problems connected with the subject. This same impression was on loan to the Boston Museum at that time. It is now clear that this very rare impression was printed after transfer to a second stone between 1881 and 1893. All traces of the original stones were lost before the turn of the century.

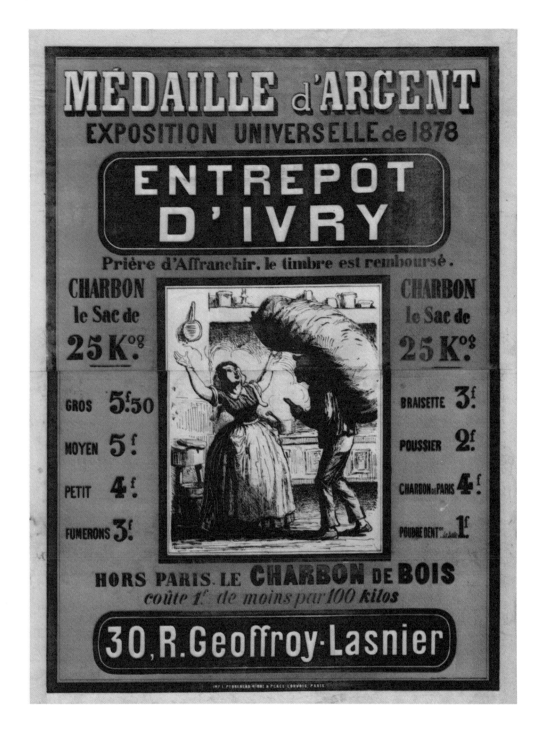

Wood engravings and etching

178

LE BAISER
The Kiss

Wood engraving
Signed l.r.; F.L. Schmied après H. Daumier 11/25
F.L. Schmied, after a drawing by Daumier in the Louvre

179

INTÉRIEUR D'UN OMNIBUS
Interior of an omnibus

Wood engraving, 1864
B. 943
F.L. Schmied impression 11/25
Re-impression Meynial, 1930, Paris

180

EXPOSITION DE PEINTURES ET DESSINS
de Daumier — Les fauteuils d'orchestre
*Exhibition of paintings and drawings by Daumier —
The orchestra seats*

Wood engraving, 1878
Signed left: A. Lepère; right: H. Daumier
B. 991
F.L. Schmied impression 11/25
Re-impression Meynial, 1930, Paris

The exhibition of the works of Daumier was organized for the benefit of the artist by his friends. It opened in 1878 at the gallery of Durand-Ruel. The plate of Lapère is from the last wood block engraved while the artist was still alive. A watercolor of the same subject was formerly in the Gerstenberg Collection, New York.

181a

LE GALOP FASHIONABLE DU GRAND-SALON
à la courtille
The fashionable rush through the showroom at the public garden

Wood engraving
B. 62

181b

LE MONDE DU DIMANCHE AUX TUILERIES
Sunday strollers in the Tuileries

"Chroniques de Paris," 1834-1835
Wood engraving
B. 81
1839

182

JEAN QUI PLEURE
Jean qui rit
John who cries
John who laughs

"Chroniques de Paris," 1834-1835
Wood engravings
B. 50-51
Reissued in *Petit Journal Pour Rire*

183

ESSAI D'EAU FORTE
Head of a man

Del. 3955
1872

The small head of a man in the upper left corner of the plate represents Daumier's only known etching. It was made after a dinner party in the home of a friend, Charles de Beriot. Three other artists who were present, Félicien Rops, Alfred Taiée and Harpignies also had contributed a small composition. The print was later published as a frontispiece to the catalogue by J.F. Champfleury of Daumier's first exhibition, in 1878, at Durand-Ruel in Paris.

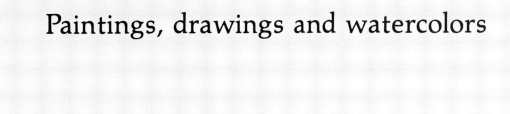

Paintings, drawings and watercolors

184

LES AVOCATS
The Lawyers (The Bar) ca. 1860

Oil on canvas (32.5 x 50.0 cm)
Signed lower right

Collections: Corot, Geoffroy-Dechaume, Bureau.

Exhibitions: Paris, *Durand-Ruel*, 1878, no. 39; Paris, *La Caricature*, 1888, no. 34; Paris, *Exposition Internationale Universelle*, 1900, no. 186; Paris, *Beaux Arts*, 1901, no. 17; Atlanta, Denver, Buffalo, Edinburgh, Oslo, Stockholm, *The Armand Hammer Collection*, 1977-1979; Los Angeles, Los Angeles County Museum of Art, *Daumier in Retrospect, 1808-1879*, Mar. 20-June 3, 1979, no. 184; Washington, D.C., Corcoran Gallery of Art, *Daumier in Retrospect, 1808-1879*, Sept. 21, 1979-Jan. 13, 1980, no. 184; Mexico City, Cloister of Sor Juana, *Honoré Daumier y su siglo, 1808-1879*, Apr. 17-June 15, 1980, no. 184; London, Royal Academy of Arts, *Honoré Daumier 1808-1879, The Armand Hammer Daumier Collection*, Jan.-Mar. 1981.

Literature: *Catalogue de la vente, Collection Paticulière Corot*, Paris 1875, no. 664; *Alexandre*, pp. 355-56 and 375; *Catalogue de la vente, Geoffroy-Dechaume*, Paris 1893, no. 23; Klossowski 110; *Catalogue de la vente P. Bureau*, Paris 1927, no. 98; *L'Amour de L'art*, 1927, p. 155; Fuchs 20b; *Eschollier* 1930, pl. 19; Scheiwiller, pl. XX; Roger-Marx, p. 30; Feischmann/Sachs, pl. 21; Adhémar, pl. 127.

Alexander tells a charming story about Gambetta's comments, when the famous statesman — once a lawyer himself — saw the painting at the exhibition held at the Galerie Durand-Ruel in 1878. Gambetta claimed that in the painting he recognized several of his onetime colleagues, but Geoffroy-Dechaume, who accompanied Gambetta, alleged that Daumier had not set foot in a law court for the last ten years, and that these were mere creatures of his imagination, and not actual people, but the prototype of the "Lawyer" as seen by Daumier... "He knows lawyers better than they do themselves. That is why the resemblance seems so striking." (Maison excerpt)

185

DON QUIXOTE Y SANCHO PANZA
Don Quixote and Sancho Panza 1866-68

Oil on canvas (40.2 x 33.0 cm)
Signed lower left: h.D.

Collections: Ferdinand Roybet, Paris; Paul Selignon, Paris, gift of Roybet, 1880; Maurice Goldblatt, New York City, 1924; Julius Weitzner, New York City, 1927; Dr. Franz H. Hirschland, Harrison, New York, 1927-1978; Eugene Thaw, New York City, 1978; Artemis (David Garritt, London), 1980.

Exhibitions: New York, Museum of Modern Art, *Corot-Daumier*, Oct. 16-Nov. 23, 1930, no. 52, repr. in cat.; Chicago, The Art Institute, *A Century of Progress, Exhibition of Paintings and Sculpture*, June 1-Nov. 1, 1934, no. 181 in cat.; Springfield, Mass., Museum of Fine Arts, extended loan prior to 1940; Mexico City, Cloister of Sor Juana, *Honoré Daumier y su siglo, 1808-1879*, Apr. 17-June 15, 1980, no. 185; London, Royal Academy of Arts, *Honoré Daumier 1808-1879, The Armand Hammer Daumier Collection*, Jan.-Mar. 1981.

Literature: Eduard Fuchs, *Der Maler Daumier*, Munich: A. Langen, 1927, no. 303, repr.; K.E. Maison, *Honoré Daumier, Catalogue Raisonné of the Paintings, Watercolours and Drawings*, London: Thames and Hudson, 1968, vol. I, p. 164, no. 1-206, repr. pl. 162; L. Barzini and G. Mandel, *L'Opera Pittorica Completa di Daumier*, Milan: Rizzoli, 1971, p. 111, no. 265, repr.

185
DON QUIXOTE Y SANCHO PANZA

To the Romantic artists of the nineteenth century, Don Quixote, knight-errant in fantasy, was not a ridiculous mock-hero but a real yet tragic hero, who like themselves was misunderstood and rejected by society. He thus became the sympathetic subject of painters from Delacroix to Daubigny and Corot. For the literary critics of the 1860s the tall, emaciated Knight of La Mancha on his skeletal steed, ready to make every sacrifice for his dreams and illusions, and his rotund squire, Sancho Panza, for whom human comforts were aspirations enough, embodied the antithesis of idealism and realism. Daumier's paintings and drawings of Don Quixote and Sancho Panza incorporate both of these interpretations, but are not restricted to them; for Daumier's images are so free of limiting narrative and descriptive detail that they permit interpretations as boundless as those of Cervantes' novel.

The Hammer *Don Quixote and Sancho Panza* is the most classic of Daumier's paintings of the Knight and his squire riding into the canvas from the darkness of the mountain night to the brilliance of the new day. The rocky landscape in the foreground opens upon a broad sunny valley toward which the protagonists descend. The bulky figure of Sancho, giving weight to the foreground, sleeps astride the donkey, incapable of understanding or sharing in his master's lofty dedication. Don Quixote, high in the saddle like a St. George, with lance raised, calmly looks out over the valley, ready for whatever unknown perils it may hold, whatever noble deeds it may require of him — a heroic figure in a heroic landscape. The sky is not that of sunset towards which old warriors traditionally face, but of sunrise that holds the future. Is Daumier's interest here in the many dualities of human nature embodied in the Knight and his squire, or is it in part autobiographical, recalling his own early years of tilting with the windmills in the Chamber of Deputies and the giants and enchanters of oppressive government as well as his lifelong good-humored satirization of Sancho's French counterparts who were also part of himself?

No other literary figures so fascinated Daumier as did Don Quixote and Sancho Panza. He painted and drew them a few times separately but much more frequently as a pair, sharing one of their recorded adventures or resting or riding together. Maison reproduces thirty-five drawings (vol. II, pls. 139-151), without dating, and twenty-nine paintings (vol. I, pls. 146-169 and 198) which he dates between 1847-48 and 1870-73, twenty of them between 1864-65 and 1868-70.

Among the latter are the five typologically related paintings of Don Quixote and Sancho Panza in the mountains. Two, dated by Maison 1864-65, are earlier than the Hammer version; two are a bit later. In the earlier paintings — Burrell Collection, Glasgow City Corporation; heirs of Herman Schulman, Israel — the mountain which occupies three-quarters of the painting is a barrier to be overcome and what lies beyond is unknown. In the Glasgow painting the contrasts are somewhat intensified by the darkening of the pigments over the century; the earthly Sancho is almost absorbed into the landscape, while the ethereal Knight, high above Sancho, ascends as in a Baroque apotheosis to the glory of the sunrise.

Maison's proposed date for the Hammer picture is 1866-68. The two slightly later pictures, one in the collection of Dr. Oskar Reinhart, Winterthur, the other in the Nationalgalerie, Berlin are both unfinished; the latter was completed by another artist to the point that only Don Quixote and his horse are by Daumier's hand. They are quite different from the Hammer picture in conception, being concerned at least in their incomplete states with the movement of forms and colors.

Daumier's lack of technical knowledge of painting, often resulted not only in deterioration but in repeated restoration, beginning in the artist's lifetime. The excellence of the condition of the Hammer painting is, therefore, quite exceptional.

The first owner of the Hammer *Don Quixote and Sancho Panza*, Ferdinand Roybet (1840-1920) was a successful academic artist in Paris, especially noted for his costume pieces. Since he is recorded as having given the painting to Paul Selignon in 1880, the year following Daumier's death, he must have acquired it directly from the artist or from his estate.

237

LA LEÇON DE LECTURE (LA LECTURE)

237*

LA LEÇON DE LECTURE (LA LECTURE)
The Reading Lesson ca. 1857

Oil on panel (27.0 x 22.0 cm)
Signed lower right: h.D.

Collections: Durand-Ruel, Paris (1890); George Vanderbilt, New York; Durand-Ruel, New York; Mrs. Edith Stuyvesant-Gerry, Providence, R.I.; George H.V. Cecil, Asheville, North Carolina.

Exhibition: London, Royal Academy of Arts, *Honoré Daumier 1808-1879, The Armand Hammer Daumier Collection*, Jan.-Mar. 1981.

Literature: Erich Klossowski, *Honoré Daumier*, 2nd ed., Munich 1923, p. 309, repr. pl. 122; Arsène Alexandre, *Honoré Daumier — L'Homme et l'Oeuvre*, 2nd ed., Paris 1928, repr. pl. 19; Eduard Fuchs, *Der Maler Daumier*, 2nd ed., Munich 1930, repr. pl. 276a; Jacques Laissaigne, *Daumier*, Paris 1938, repr. pl. 40; Curt Schweicher, *Daumier*, London 1954, repr. pl. 4; K.E. Maison, *Honoré Daumier, Catalogue Raisonné of the Paintings, Watercolours and Drawings*, London: Thames and Hudson, 1968, vol. I, p. 106, no. I-102, repr. pl. 74; Luigi Barzini and Gabriele Mandel, *L'Opera Pittorica Completa di Daumier*, Milan: Rizzoli, 1971, no. 131, repr.; Sale catalogue: *Impressionist and Modern Paintings and Sculptures*, New York: Sotheby Parke Bernet, Inc., May 13, 1980, no. 207, repr.

*Recent acquisition

In most histories of art, Daumier is classified along with Courbet and Millet as an exponent of the new mid-nineteenth century realism based on the actualities of daily existence. *The Reading Lesson* exemplifies the extent to which he is also heir to the centuries old French tradition of idealized realism.

The Reading Lesson is part of an extensive group of Daumier paintings of varied formal and psychological relationships between two or more persons engaged in cultivated urbane activities such as reading, singing, looking at works of art, attending the theater or playing chess. The figures in this group are usually common types, but they are individualized through details of physiognomy and dress which define personalities and social status. In *The Reading Lesson*, on the contrary, those very details of appearance, dress and setting are eliminated so that the figures, rather than representing characteristic mid-nineteenth century Parisians, became more classically abstract representations of "man" and "boy." The composition also has a classical unity of organization. By overlapping the heads and riveting the attention of both boy and man on the point where finger meets book, Daumier has achieved here a closer unity between the two figures than in any related subject. In a manner consonant with classical usage, he shows each figure at the height of emotional involvement in the subject: the boy with eager attention, the man with monk-like engrossment. The resultant images in this and a number of other works by Daumier are those of the "honnête homme," the simple human being fulfilling his role in life with dignity. These works place Daumier in a continuous line of development from Louis LeNain in the seventeenth century through Chardin in the eighteenth.

If the composition of *The Reading Lesson* recalls an early seventeenth century St. Matthew and the Angel, the technique anticipates the Blue Period of Picasso.

In a revolutionary way Daumier abandoned verisimilitude and smooth surfaces for expressive line and clearly perceptible forms. In *The Reading Lesson*, he first indicated shapes by outlines drawn with the brush. He then built up volumes within the outlines with overlapping pigments and glazes, almost as if he were working in terracotta. Finally, he strengthened the outlines and delineated the features with surface lines.

Maison dates *The Reading Lesson* about 1857. External evidence for dating Daumier paintings is available for only eight: his only dated picture, *The Laundress*, 1863, in the Metropolitan Museum of Art in New York; *La Republique*, painted for a competition in 1848; and six oils that he submitted to Salon exhibitions between 1849 and 1869. Further complicating the matter, Daumier often set aside works to be completed at a later date and a number of them were finished by others after his death. By combining intensive research into Daumier's technique and style with the sparse existing evidence, Daumier specialists have been able to establish a chronology for approximately three hundred paintings and to propose a logical development of his style.

The Reading Lesson is typical of Daumier's middle period, the 1850s, when he was vigorously investigating form and psychological content. The *Don Quixote and Sancho Panza* in the Hammer Collection is representative of his time of greatest inventiveness and technical maturity: the 1860s and early 1870s. Both works have been accepted without question by Daumier scholars as entirely by Daumier's hand.

239*

SCÈNE DE COMÉDIE

Two Actors ca. 1870-73

Oil on panel (24.7 x 31.8 cm)

Collections: Mme Henry Marcel; Wildenstein and Co., Paris and New York; R.W. Redford; Wildenstein and Co., New York; Mr. & Mrs. André Meyer, New York.

Exhibitions: Paris, Musée de l'Orangerie, *Daumier: Peintures, Aquarelles, Dessins,* 1934, no. 32; Washington, D.C., National Gallery of Art, *Exhibition of the Collection of Mr. and Mrs. André Meyer,* 1962, p. 14, repr.; New York, Wildenstein and Co., *Romantics and Realists,* 1966; London, Royal Academy of Arts, *Honoré Daumier 1808-1879, The Armand Hammer Daumier Collection,* Jan.-Mar. 1981.

Literature: André Fontainas, *La Peinture de Daumier,* 1923, repr. pl. 20; Eduard Fuchs, *Der Maler Daumier,* Munich 1927, repr. pl. 126; Jacques Lassaigne, *Daumier,* 1938, repr. pl. 140; Curt Schweicher, *Daumier,* 1954, repr. pl. 52; K.E. Maison, *Honoré Daumier, Catalogue Raisonné of the Paintings, Watercolours and Drawings,* London: Thames and Hudson, 1968, vol. I, p. 181, no. I-237, repr. pl. 144; Luigi Barzini and Gabriel Mandel, *L'Opera Pittorica Completa di Daumier,* Milan: Rizzoli, 1971, no. 299, repr. p. 113; Sale catalogue: *Highly Important Paintings, Drawings and Sculpture from the André Meyer Collection,* New York: Sotheby Parke Bernet, Inc., Oct. 22, 1980, no. 13, repr. opp.

*Recent acquisition

In the later years of this life, Daumier's style became progressively more painterly with greater freedom, fluidity and exploitation of the expressive powers of the painting medium. Daumier's delight in the texture of paint and movement of the brush can indeed be noted in *Two Actors*, dated by scholars between 1870 and 1873. Maison aptly described it as "an outstandingly beautiful late study of the footlights' effect on two actors, probably from a play by Molière."

While the individual characters in *Two Actors* have not been identified, the suggestion of a Molière play has considerable basis. When Daumier was asked who was his master in art, he reportedly replied: "Molière." Daumier and Molière shared a delight in exaggerating accordingly those human characteristics which they approved or disdained in order that the public regard their subjects with acclaim or disgrace. Daumier had seen Molière's work at the Comédie Française and his is the kind of world portrayed in *Two Actors*. There is a bravura in the stance of the foreground figure and also a sweep of the brush recalling the flamboyant portraits by Fragonard such as *Portrait of an Actor* in the Louvre or *Portrait of a Warrier* in Williamstown. At the same time, the character and emotions of the actors evoked by use of color and distortion provide a rationale for Daumier's influence on twentieth century expressionists.

240

LES AMATEURS DE TABLEAUX

240*

LES AMATEURS DE TABLEAUX

The Picture Connoisseurs ca. 1858-62

Oil on panel (33.2 x 23.5 cm)

Collections: Ambroise Vollard, Paris; Jacques Dubourg, Paris; Galerie Matthiesen; R. Oppenheimer; Paul Rosenberg and Co., New York; Galerie Alex Maguy, Paris.

Exhibitions: Paris, Bibliothèque Nationale, *Daumier, Le Peintre Graveur*, 1958, no. 219; London, Arts Council of Great Britain, Tate Gallery, *Daumier, Paintings and Drawings*, 1961, no. 52; London, Royal Academy of Arts, *Honoré Daumier 1808-1879, The Armand Hammer Daumier Collection*, Jan.-Mar. 1981.

Literature: K.E. Maison, "Some Unpublished Works by Daumier," *Gazette des Beaux-Arts* May-June, 1958, p. 342-4 and fig. 3; K.E. Maison, *Honoré Daumier, Catalogue Raisonné of the Paintings, Watercolours and Drawings*, London: Thames and Hudson, 1968, vol. I, p. 121, no. I-131, repr. pl. 88; Luigi Barzini and Gabriel Mandel, *L'Opera Pittorica Completa di Daumier*, Milan: Rizzoli, 1971, p. 103, no. 80; Sale catalogue: *Impressionist and Modern Paintings and Sculpture*, New York: Sotheby Parke Bernet, Inc., Oct. 22, 1980, no. 42, repr. opp.

This version of *Les Amateurs de Tableaux* is not only "a bold and most powerful *tour-de-force*," as Maison described it, but also a valuable document of Daumier's working method. It is the first oil sketch for the 40.0 x 32.5 cm painting, formerly in the collection of Mrs. Harris Jones, New York. Daumier's first annotation was a small charcoal sketch of the three full figures in which he explored the compositional structure; next was the Hammer sketch in which he studied the light (presumably from a skylight beyond at upper left) that produced sharp highlights against the limited room illumination. Then followed a second oil sketch of the full composition further integrating light and structure; and finally a compositional drawing in which the space was expanded, background figures added and the three men drawn into a closer unit as in the final painting. A growing psychological unity parallels the increasing structural unity in the five versions. All are reproduced in Maison's catalogue. The setting is the great auction house, the Hôtel Drouot.

The Hammer *Amateurs* is a typical middle period Daumier with its "Rembrandtesque" chiaroscuro, its use of color and its technique of heavy brush outlining of figures to be filled in to make solid sculptural forms. Although the painting had belonged to Ambroise Vollard, it was unknown to scholars and the public until 1958 when Jean Adhémar included it in the Daumier 150th anniversary exhibition at the Bibliothèque Nationale in Paris and K.E. Maison published it in the *Gazette des Beaux-Arts*. Maison characterized its condition as "mint state of preservation."

*Recent acquisition

241*

TÊTE DE SONNEUR
Head of a Bell-ringer ca. 1865-66

Oil on panel (35.0 x 27.0 cm)
Signed lower right: h.D.

Collections: Boulard; Arsène Alexandre (sale, Paris, 1903, no. 23); Frau von D...
(sale, Munich, Helbing, 1912, no. 15); Leicester Galleries, London; Margaret S. Davies;
Private collection, Yorkshire, England, 1960.

Exhibitions: Paris, L'Ecole des Beaux-Arts, *Exposition Daumier*, 1901, no. 4; London,
Leicester Galleries, *Honoré Daumier*, 1936, no. 85; Cardiff and Swansea, Arts Council
of Great Britain, *Daumier-Millet-Courbet*, 1957, no. 5; London, Arts Council of Great
Britain, Tate Gallery, *Daumier, Paintings and Drawings*, 1961, no. 43; London, Royal
Academy of Arts, *Honoré Daumier 1808-1879, The Armand Hammer Daumier Collection*,
Jan.-Mar. 1981.

Literature: Erich Klossowski, *Honoré Daumier*, Munich: R. Piper Co., 1923, no. 237,
repr. pl. 128; Eduard Fuchs, *Der Maler Daumier*, Munich: A. Langen, 1927, no. 17b;
Jacques Laissaigne, *Daumier*, Paris: Hyperion, 1938, repr. pl. 34; Jean Adhémar, *Honoré
Daumier*, Paris 1954, repr. pl. 86; Curt Schweicher, *Daumier*, London 1954, repr. pl. 5;
Sale catalogue, London: Sotheby & Co., May 4, 1960, no. 106 (Property of Miss
Margaret S. Davies); K.E. Maison, *Honoré Daumier, Catalogue Raisonné of the Paintings,
Watercolours and Drawings*, London: Thames and Hudson, 1968, vol. I, p. 156, no. I-191,
repr. pl. 21; Sale catalogue: *Important Impressionist and Modern Paintings and Sculpture*,
London: Sotheby Parke Bernet, Inc., Dec. 3, 1980, no. 4, repr.

In his *Catalogue Raisonné*, K.E. Maison says: "In the catalogue of the exhibition at the
Tate Gallery, 1961, I dated this picture 'not later than 1855,' however, after having
seen it against the background of the exhibition, I now believe it to be considerably
later. Adhémar's suggestion that Daumier may have met the bell-ringer of Notre-
Dame in the studio of his friend Geoffroy-Dechaume is very plausible; it was situated
in the immediate vicinity of the cathedral. Nevertheless, the picture was not painted
as a portrait from life."

*Recent acquisition

241
TÊTE DE SONNEUR

186
UN AVOCAT PLAIDANT

UN AVOCAT PLAIDANT
The Pleading Lawyer

Watercolor ink and gouache (15.9 x 21.6 cm)

Collections: Bellino (sale, Paris, 1892, no. 32); H.P. (sale, Paris, 1901, no. 5); Paul Gallimard, Paris; Paul Cassirer, Berlin; Jakob Goldschmidt, Berlin and New York; Alfred E. Goldschmidt, Stamford, Conn.

Exhibitions: Paris, Palais du Louvre, *Exposition de Tableaux, Statues et Objects d'Arts, au Profit de l'Oeuvre des Orphelins d'Alsace Lorraine*, 1885, no. 101 (lent by Bellino); Paris, L'Ecole des Beaux-Arts, *Exposition des Peintures, Aquarelles, Dessins et Lithographies des Maîtres de la Caricature, et de la Peinture de Moeurs au XIXème Siècle*, 1888, no. 392; Paris, Exposition Universelle, *Exposition Centennale de l'Art Français*, 1889, no. 135 (lent by Bellino); Paris, Galerie L. and P. Rosenberg, *Exposition de Dessins, Aquarelles et Lithographies de Honoré Daumier*, Apr. 15-May 6, 1907 (lent by Gallimard); St. Petersbourg, *L'Art Français, Exposition Centennale*, Jan. 15-28, 1912, no. 3 (lent by Jakob Goldschmidt); Berlin, Galerie Paul Cassirer, *Ein Jahrhundert Französischer Zeichnung*, Dec. 1929-Jan. 1930, no. 17; London, Matthiesen Gallery, *A Century of French Drawings*, May 3-21, 1938, no. 39; London, Tate Gallery, The Arts Council of Great Britain, *Daumier — Paintings and Drawings*, June 14-July 30, 1961, no. 223 (lent by Mr. and Mrs. A.E. Goldschmidt); Little Rock, San Francisco, Oklahoma City, San Diego, Los Angeles, London, Dublin, Leningrad, Moscow, Kiev, Minsk, Riga, Odessa, Caracas, Lima, Tokyo, Kyoto, Fukuoka, Nagoya, Nashville, Mexico City, Paris, Malibu, Atlanta, Denver, Buffalo, Edinburgh, Oslo, Stockholm, *The Armand Hammer Collection*, 1970-1979; Los Angeles, Los Angeles County Museum of Art, *Daumier in Retrospect, 1808-1879*, Mar. 20-June 3, 1979, no. 185; Washington, D.C., Corcoran Gallery of Art, *Daumier in Retrospect, 1808-1879*, Sept. 21, 1979-Jan. 13, 1980, no. 185; Mexico City, Cloister of Sor Juana, *Honoré Daumier y su siglo, 1808-1879*, Apr. 17-June 15, 1980, no. 186; London, Royal Academy of Arts, *Honoré Daumier 1808-1879, The Armand Hammer Daumier Collection*, Jan.-Mar. 1981.

Literature: L'Ecole des Beaux-Arts, *Catalogue de l'Exposition des Peintures, Aquarelles, Dessins et Lithographies des Maîtres Français de la Caricature*, Paris: Maison Quantin, 1888 (Préface Paul Mantz), *Gazette des Beaux-Arts*, no. 392, p. 85; Armand Dayot, *Un Siècle d'Art, Notes sur la Peinture Française à l'Exposition Centennale des Beaux-Arts, Catalogue Complet des Oeuvres Exposées*, Paris: Librairie Plon. 1890, p. 150; René Jean, *Catalogue Commemoratif, L'Art Français à Saint-Petersbourg*, Exposition Centennale, Paris: Goupil et Cie, Manzi-Joyant et Cie, 1912, no. 3, p. 34; Erich Klossowski, *Honoré Daumier*, Munich: R. Piper Co., 1923, no. 177b, p. 102; Eduard Fuchs, *Der Maler Daumier*, New York: E. Weyhe, Leipzig: Hesse & Backet, 1927, and 1930, no. 198a, p. 54, repr. pl. 198; K.E. Maison, *Daumier Drawings*, New York and London: Thomas Yoseloff, 1960, no. 134, p. 29, repr. pl. 134; Arts Council of Great Britain, *Catalogue of an Exhibition of Daumier Paintings and Drawings at the Tate Gallery*, London: Curwen Press, 1961, no. 223, p. 67; K.E. Maison, *Honoré Daumier, Catalogue Raisonné of the Paintings, Watercolours and Drawings*, London: Thames and Hudson, 1968, vol. II, no. 675, repr. pl. 259; Sale catalogue: *Important Impressionist and Modern Paintings and Drawings*, New York: Sotheby Parke Bernet, Inc., Oct. 28, 1970, no. 13, p. 24, repr. opp.

The legal profession was one which allowed Daumier the full vent of his piercing satire. He scarcely made a study of that occupation which did not expose its hypocrisy, rapacity and stentorian oratory. At the same time, these devastating interpretations were cushioned by the artist's overriding comic sense with the result that lawyers and judges became objects of laughter rather than of derision and scorn.

The Hammer watercolor is a rare example of a Daumier interpretation of a lawyer, in that it is not risible but, on the contrary, almost sympathetic. The subject is an old, buck-toothed pleader who is shown in an intense, impassioned moment which seems to embody a lifetime of courtroom behavior and to capture the timelessness of ingrained custom. Light illuminates the intent, even earnest, wrinkled face, its expression molded by constant harangue, silhouettes the semaphoric right hand, and falls sensitively on the knuckles of the other in which the brief is clasped. The head, so intensely realistic that one can almost hear the lawyer's words, is drawn with Daumier's unique lineality, composed of s-curves, arcs, parentheses, and other generally serpentine strophes, deftly but economically applied. The scene is completed with watercolor, the robes and hat heightened with gouache. Daumier fully signed the work which, although relatively small, is a highly finished masterpiece among his legal subjects.

The difficulty of arriving at an exact chronology for many of Daumier's drawings and watercolors has been pointed out repeatedly. K.E. Maison suggested that the time span between "early" and "late" works in Daumier's oeuvre may be as much as twenty-five years. A systematic or consistent evolution in the artist's drawings appears improbable, and his studies and sketches defy definite dating.

Although the Hammer drawing has not been dated by Maison, a reasonable or justifiable chronology for Daumier's large group of drawings of legal subjects may be suggested by their apparent relationship to the thirty-nine lithographs, *Les Gens de Justice*, which were printed in *Le Charivari* from 1845 to 1848. Jean Adhémar has placed many paintings, drawings and watercolors of legal subjects in the period of 1843 to 1846 although he dates a spirited drawing, *Lawyer*, in the Boymans Museum as late as about 1865. Maison places a drawing, *Les deux avocats*, in 1860.

187

UN WAGON DE TROISIÈME CLASSE
Third Class Carriage

Red chalk on blue paper (26.7 x 33.0 cm)
Unsigned

Collections: Roger Marx, Paris; Strolin, Paris; Hirshland, New York; Myrtil Frank, New York.

Exhibitions: Paris, Malibu, Atlanta, Denver, Buffalo, Edinburgh, Oslo, Stockholm, *The Armand Hammer Collection, 1977-1979*; Los Angeles, Los Angeles County Museum of Art, *Daumier in Retrospect, 1808-1879*, Mar. 20-June 3, 1979, no. 186; Washington, D.C., Corcoran Gallery of Art, *Daumier in Retrospect, 1808-1879*, Sept. 21, 1979-Jan. 13, 1980, no. 186; Mexico City, Cloister of Sor Juana, *Honoré Daumier y su siglo, 1808-1879*, Apr. 17-June 15, 1980, no. 187; London, Royal Academy of Arts, *Honoré Daumier 1808-1879, The Armand Hammer Daumier Collection*, Jan.-Mar. 1981.

Literature: *Catalogue de la vente Roger Marx*, Paris 1914, II, no. 108; Erich Klossowski, *Honoré Daumier*, Munich 1923, no. 258c; K.E. Maison, *Honoré Daumier, Catalogue Raisonné of the Paintings, Watercolours and Drawings*, London: Thames and Hudson, 1968, vol. II, no. 287, ill. pl. 74.

Note: This drawing is very close (in reverse) to the painting I-178 in Maison; the painting, however, shows the traveler's hand resting on his knees.

188

DEUX FEMMES ET UN ENFANT
Two Women and a Child

Pen and brown and black wash, heightened with white chalk (21.0 x 18.0 cm)
Initialed

Exhibitions: Paris, Durand-Ruel, 1878, no. 123; Paris, Beaux-Arts, 1901, no. 160; Malibu, Atlanta, Denver, Buffalo, Edinburgh, Oslo, Stockholm, *The Armand Hammer Collection,* 1977-1979; Los Angeles, Los Angeles County Museum of Art, *Daumier in Retrospect, 1808-1879*, Mar. 20-June 3, 1979, no. 187; Washington, D.C., Corcoran Gallery of Art, *Daumier in Retrospect, 1808-1879*, Sept. 21, 1979-Jan. 13, 1980, no. 187; Mexico City, Cloister of Sor Juana, *Honoré Daumier y su siglo, 1808-1879*, Apr. 17-June 15, 1980, no. 188; London, Royal Academy of Arts, *Honoré Daumier 1808-1879, The Armand Hammer Daumier Collection*, Jan.-Mar. 1981.

It has repeatedly been suggested that this drawing may represent the Virgin holding the Infant Christ, with Saint Anne.

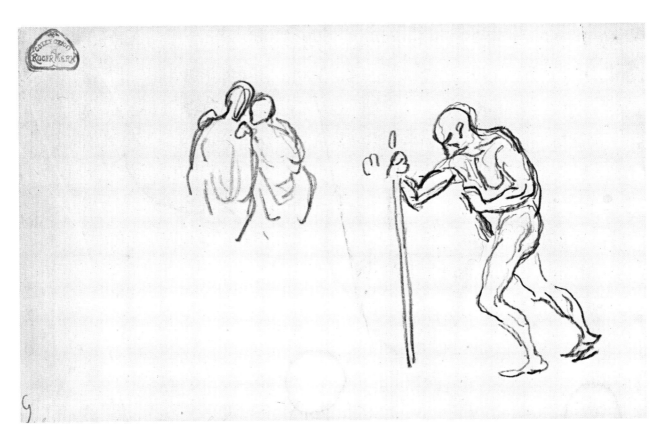

189

UN HOMME AU BATON
Man with a Staff

Pencil (25.5 x 31.0 cm)

Exhibitions: Los Angeles, Los Angeles County Museum of Art, *Daumier in Retrospect, 1808-1879*, Mar. 20-June 3, 1979, no. 188; Washington, D.C., Corcoran Gallery of Art, *Daumier in Retrospect, 1808-1879*, Sept. 21, 1979-Jan. 13, 1980, no. 188; Mexico City, Cloister of Sor Juana, *Honoré Daumier y su siglo, 1808-1879*, Apr. 17-June 15, 1980, no. 189; London, Royal Academy of Arts, *Honoré Daumier 1808-1879, The Armand Hammer Daumier Collection*, Jan.-Mar. 1981.

190

LE SALTIMBANQUE ET L'ÉCUYÈRE
Mountebank and Squire

Pencil and sanguine over charcoal (32.2 x 25.8 cm)

Collection: Maurice Loncle, Paris.

Exhibitions: Paris, 1958, Bibliothèque Nationale, no. 204; Paris, Musée Cognacq-Jay, *Daumier*, no. 17; Los Angeles, Los Angeles County Museum of Art, *Daumier in Retrospect, 1808-1879*, Mar. 20-June 3, 1979, no. 189; Washington, D.C., Corcoran Gallery of Art, *Daumier in Retrospect, 1808-1879*, Sept. 21, 1979-Jan. 13, 1980, no. 189; Mexico City, Cloister of Sor Juana, *Honoré Daumier y su siglo, 1808-1879*, Apr. 17-June 15, 1980, no. 190; London, Royal Academy of Arts, *Honoré Daumier 1808-1879, The Armand Hammer Daumier Collection*, Jan.-Mar. 1981.

Literature: K.E. Maison, *Honoré Daumier, Catalogue Raisonné of the Paintings, Watercolours and Drawings*, London: Thames and Hudson, 1968, vol. II, p. 176, no. 529, repr. pl. 186.

191

ÉTUDE DE TÊTES

Study of Heads

Charcoal (16.5 x 21.6 cm)

Collection: Paul Bureau, Paris.

Exhibitions: Paris, L'Ecole des Beaux Arts, *Exposition Daumier*, 1901, no. 165; Paris, Bibliothèque Nationale, *Daumier, Le Peintre Graveur*, 1958, no. 173; Washington, D.C., Corcoran Gallery of Art, *Daumier in Retrospect, 1808-1879*, Sept. 21, 1979-Jan. 13, 1980, no. 187; Mexico City, Cloister of Sor Juana, *Honoré Daumier y su siglo, 1808-1879*, Apr. 17-June 15, 1980, no. 188; London, Royal Academy of Arts, *Honoré Daumier 1808-1879, The Armand Hammer Daumier Collection*, Jan.-Mar. 1981.

Literature: K.E. Maison, *Honoré Daumier, Catalogue Raisonné of the Paintings, Watercolours and Drawings*, London: Thames and Hudson, 1968, vol. II, no. 164, pl. 33.

192

FEUILLES D'ÉTUDES, AU PALAIS DE JUSTICE
Studies at the Palace of Justice after 1846

Pen and ink (29.2 x 40.6 cm)

Collection: Roger Marx, Paris; Claude Roger Marx, Paris.

Exhibitions: Paris, Gallerie Dru, *Aquarelles et Dessins de Daumier*, 1927, no. 61; Paris, Musee de l'Orangerie, *Daumier: Peintures Aquarelles Dessins*, 1934, no. 126; London, The Leicester Galleries, *Paintings Drawings and Lithographs by Honoré Daumier*, 1936, no. 47; Vienna, Albertina, *H. Daumier Ausstellung: Zeichnungen, Aquarelle, Lithographien und Klein Plastiken*, 1936, no. 51; Washington, D.C., Corcoran Gallery of Art, *Daumier in Retrospect, 1808-1879*, Sept. 21, 1979-Jan. 13, 1980, no. 187; Mexico City, Cloister of Sor Juana, *Honoré Daumier y su siglo, 1808-1879*, Apr. 17-June 15, 1980, no. 188; London, Royal Academy of Arts, *Honoré Daumier 1808-1879, The Armand Hammer Daumier Collection*, Jan.-Mar. 1981.

Literature: K.E. Maison, *Honoré Daumier, Catalogue Raisonné of the Paintings, Watercolours and Drawings*, London: Thames and Hudson, 1968, vol. II, no. 616, pl. 233.

193

UN AVOCAT PLAIDANT	DEUX ÉTUDES D'UN ABOYEUR
A Pleading Lawyer — recto ca. 1866	*Two Studies of a Barker* — verso
Charcoal, pen and India ink (120.0 x 23.8 cm)	Charcoal

Collections: M. Joyant, Paris; Maurice Loncle, Paris.

Exhibitions: Paris, Bibliothèque Nationale, *Daumier, Le Peintre Graveur*, 1958, no. 169; Paris, Musée Cognacq-Jay, *Daumier*, 1961, no. 16; Washington, D.C., Corcoran Gallery of Art, *Daumier in Retrospect, 1808-1879*, Sept. 21, 1979-Jan. 13, 1980, no. 187; Mexico City, Cloister of Sor Juana, *Honoré Daumier y su siglo, 1808-1879*, Apr. 17-June 15, 1980, no. 188; London, Royal Academy of Arts, *Honoré Daumier 1808-1879, The Armand Hammer Daumier Collection*, Jan.-Mar. 1981.

Literature: K.E. Maison, *Honoré Daumier, Catalogue Raisonné of the Paintings, Watercolours and Drawings*, London: Thames and Hudson, 1968, vol. II, no. 626, pl. 236, *recto*; 508, pl. 175, *verso*.

194

DON QUICHOTTE DANS LES MONTAGNES
Don Quixote in the Mountains — recto ca. 1866

Charcoal and white gouache (24.0 x 43.2 cm)

Collections: M. Joyant, Paris; Maurice Loncle, Paris.

Exhibitions: Paris, Musée des Arts Décoratifs, *Un Siècle de Caricature*, 1932, no. 400; Paris, Bibliothèque Nationale, *Daumier, Le Peintre Graveur*, 1958, no. 218; London, Tate Gallery, The Arts Council of Great Britain, *Daumier Paintings and Drawings*, 1961, no. 230; Washington, D.C., Corcoran Gallery of Art, *Daumier in Retrospect, 1808-1879*, Sept. 21, 1979-Jan. 13, 1980, no. 187; Mexico City, Cloister of Sor Juana, *Honoré Daumier y su siglo, 1808-1879*, Apr. 17-June 15, 1980, no. 188; London, Royal Academy of Arts, *Honoré Daumier 1808-1879, The Armand Hammer Daumier Collection*, Jan.-Mar. 1981.

Literature: K.E. Maison, *Daumier Studies* I, in *The Burlington Magazine*, London, January 1954, p. 14, figs. 9 and 10; K.E. Maison, *Honoré Daumier, Catalogue Raisonné of the Paintings, Watercolours and Drawings*, London: Thames and Hudson, 1968, vol. II, nos. 442 and 443, pl. 149.

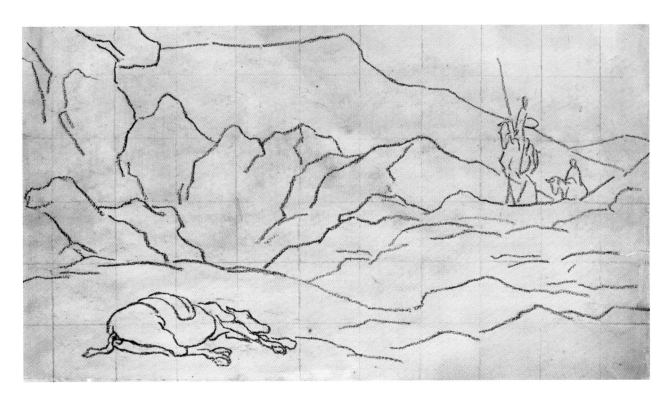

194

DON QUICHOTTE DANS LES MONTAGNES

Don Quixote in the Mountains — verso

Charcoal on paper squared for transfer

195

QUATRE HOMMES EN BUSTE
Study of Four Men

Pencil, pen and brown ink (16.2 x 25.7 cm)

Collections: Marcel Lecomte, Paris; Alex, Reid and Lefevre, London.

Exhibitions: London, Tate Gallery, The Arts Council of Great Britain, *Daumier Paintings and Drawings*, 1961, no. 171; Washington, D.C., Corcoran Gallery of Art, *Daumier in Retrospect, 1808-1879*, Sept. 21, 1979-Jan. 13, 1980, no. 187; Mexico City, Cloister of Sor Juana, *Honoré Daumier y su siglo, 1808-1879*, Apr. 17-June 15, 1980, no. 188; London, Royal Academy of Arts, *Honoré Daumier 1808-1879, The Armand Hammer Daumier Collection*, Jan.-Mar. 1981.

Literature: Honoré Daumier, *L'Autograph au Salon de 1865 et dans les Ateliers*, Paris 1865, no. 11, p. 88 (a sheet of drawings by Daumier of which two in the top row are copies of the four heads in this drawing regrouped and juxtaposed); K.E. Maison, *Daumier Drawings*, New York: Thomas Yoseloff, 1960, pl. 13; K.E. Maison, *Honoré Daumier, Catalogue Raisonné of the Paintings, Watercolours and Drawings*, London: Thames and Hudson, 1968, vol. II, no. 165, pl. 34.

vulcain

196

VULCAIN
One of the seventeen caricatures drawn by Daumier as
costume designs ca. 1853

Pen, India ink, charcoal and watercolor (27.3 x 19.0 cm)

Collections: Delphine Baron, Paris; Henri Rouart, Paris (sale, Paris Galerie Manzi-Joyant, Dec. 16, 1912, no. 61, ff. 570); M. Cottreux, Paris; Maurice Loncle, Paris; M. Gautier-Lathuille, Paris (sale, Paris, Hôtel Drouot, June 10, 1964, no. 130).

Exhibitions: Prague, *French Art*, 1956, no. 34; Paris, Bibliothèque Nationale, *Daumier, Le Peintre Graveur*, 1958, no. 148; Washington, D.C., Corcoran Gallery of Art, *Daumier in Retrospect, 1808-1879*, Sept. 21, 1979-Jan. 13, 1980, no. 187; Mexico City, Cloister of Sor Juana, *Honoré Daumier y su siglo, 1808-1879*, Apr. 17-June 15, 1980, no. 188; London, Royal Academy of Arts, *Honoré Daumier 1808-1879, The Armand Hammer Daumier Collection*, Jan.-Mar. 1981.

Literature: Erich Klossowski, *Honoré Daumier*, Munich 1923, p. 95, no. 105 N (catalogued); K.E. Maison, *Honoré Daumier, Catalogue Raisonné of the Paintings, Watercolours and Drawings*, London: Thames and Hudson, 1968, vol. II, no. 469, pl. 158.

197

LES SPECTATEURS

The Spectators — recto

Pen and India ink with gray wash (14.6 x 17.1 cm)

Collections: O. Saincere, Paris

Exhibitions: Washington, D.C., Corcoran Gallery of Art, *Daumier in Retrospect, 1808-1879*, Sept. 21, 1979-Jan. 13, 1980, no. 187; Mexico City, Cloister of Sor Juana, *Honoré Daumier y su siglo, 1808-1879*, Apr. 17-June 15, 1980, no. 188; London, Royal Academy of Arts, *Honoré Daumier 1808-1879, The Armand Hammer Daumier Collection*, Jan.-Mar. 1981.

Literature: K.E. Maison, "Some Additions to Daumier's Oeuvre," *The Burlington Magazine*, vol. CXII, Sept. 1970, p. 623, fig. 88.

197
UN COUPLE
A Couple — verso
Pen and India ink with gray wash

238*

SPECTATEURS

Spectators

Ink, crayon and wash (31.5 x 30.0 cm)

Collections: Lepoutre; Private Collection (sale, Paris, Hôtel Drouot); Private Collection (sale, Paris, Palais Galliéra).

Exhibition: London, Royal Academy of Arts, *Honoré Daumier 1808-1879, The Armand Hammer Daumier Collection*, Jan.-Mar. 1981.

Literature: Sale catalogue, Paris, Hôtel Drouot, June 12, 1929, no. 45; Klaus Fuchs, *Der Mahler Daumier*, Munich 1930, no. 327a; Sale catalogue, Paris: Palais Galliéra, May 30, 1967, no. 4; K.E. Maison, *Honoré Daumier, Catalogue Raisonné of the Paintings, Watercolours and Drawings*, London: Thames and Hudson, 1968, vol. II, no. 493, pl. 168; Sale catalogue, *Important Impressionist and Modern Paintings, Drawings and Watercolours*, London: Sotheby Parke Bernet, Inc., July 1, 1980, no. 1.

*Recent acquisition

198
DON QUICHOTTE

DON QUICHOTTE
Don Quixote

Pen and brown ink (31.4 x 23.2 cm)

Collections: Benjamin Leroux, Paris; Madame H. Leroux, Paris.

Exhibitions: Washington, D.C., Corcoran Gallery of Art, *Daumier in Retrospect, 1808-1879*, Sept. 21, 1979-Jan. 13, 1980, no. 187; Mexico City, Cloister of Sor Juana, *Honoré Daumier y su siglo, 1808-1879*, Apr. 17-June 15, 1980, no. 188; London, Royal Academy of Arts, *Honoré Daumier 1808-1879, The Armand Hammer Daumier Collection*, Jan.-Mar. 1981.

Literature: K. E. Maison, *Honoré Daumier, Catalogue Raisonné of the Paintings, Watercolours, and Drawings*, London: Thames and Hudson, 1968, vol. II, no. 423 (illustrated).

This is one of the three preliminary drawings for the *Don Quixote* paintings in the Nationalgalerie, Berlin (M. II, 52) and the Oskar Reinhart Collection, Winterthur (M. I, 207).

Sculpture

Note:

None of the bronzes in the exhibition were cast during Daumier's lifetime. The complex problems of dating the sculpture and the many technical details connected with the various castings are explored at length in the exhaustive critical and comparative study in the catalogue of Daumier's sculpture held at the Fogg Art Museum in 1969. The letter W. below each entry refers to Jean Wasserman, who edited the Fogg catalogue listed in the bibliography.

The thirty-six small busts of the Parliamentaries (cat. nos. 199 to 234) in the Hammer Collection were cast by the Barbedienne Foundry when the unbaked clay figures were in the possession of Maurice Le Garrec and his widow between the years 1929-1948.

There are only four or five collections in the world that contain an entire suite of the thirty-six bronzes from a single casting. The Hammer Collection busts are all from the thirteenth series.

The bronze figure of *Ratapoil* was cast by Alexis Rudier in 1925 in an edition of twenty. The bronze relief of *The Emigrants* is the second version of the sculpture. It was cast by Alexis Rudier in a small edition after 1952.

D'ARGOUT

Cast bronze; height 12.8 cm
Markings: MLG; inside: 13/30
(See Del. 131F)
W. 1c

200
BARTHE
Cast bronze; height 16.2 cm
Markings: MLG; inside: 13/25
(See Del. 131D)
W. 3b

CUNIN

Cast bronze; height 14.6 cm
Markings: MLG; inside: 13/25
W. 5b

202

DELORT

Cast bronze; height 23.6 cm
Markings: MLG; inside: 13/25
W. 7c

DUBOIS

Cast bronze; height 19.2 cm
Markings: MLG; inside: 13/25
W. 8c

DUPIN

Cast bronze; height 14.3 cm
Markings: MLG; inside: 13/25
W. 9d

205

ÉTIENNE

Cast bronze; height 16.2 cm
Markings: MLG; inside: 13/25
W. 10b

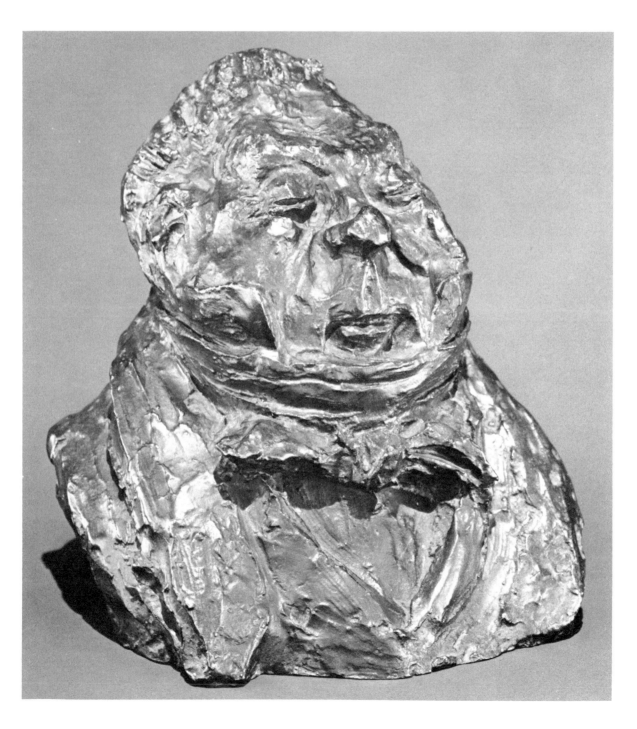

GALLOIS

Cast bronze; height 21.4 cm
Markings: MLG; inside: 13/25
W. 14c

207

GAUDRY

Cast bronze; height 16.0 cm
Markings: MLG; inside: 13/25
W. 16b

244

GUIZOT

Cast bronze; height 22.1 cm
Markings: MLG; inside: 13/30
(See Del. 131A)
W. 17c

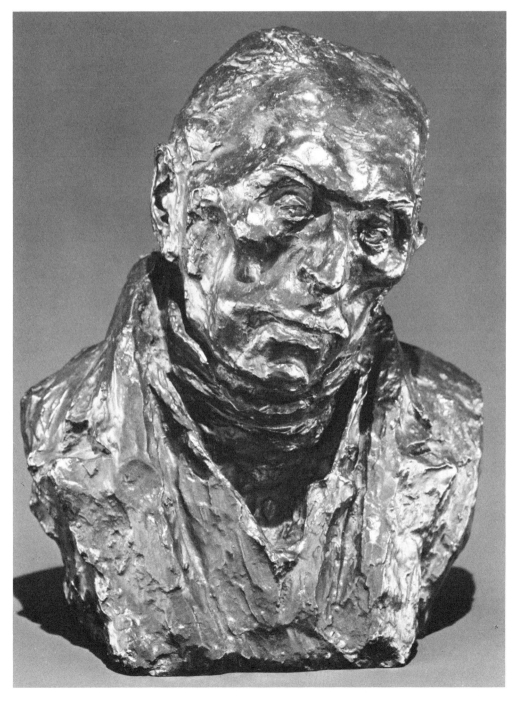

209

HARLÉ (PÈRE)

Cast bronze; height 11.9 cm
Markings: MLG; inside: 13/30
(See Del. 131K)
W. 18b

LAMETH

Cast bronze; height 14.6 cm
Markings: MLG; inside: 13/30
W. 20c

ODIER

Cast bronze; height 14.0 cm
Markings: MLG; inside: 13/30
(See Del. 131M)
W. 24b

212
PATAILLE
Cast bronze; height 16.7 cm
Markings: MLG; inside: 13/30
W. 25b

213

PRUNELLE

Cast bronze; height 16.7 cm
Markings: MLG; inside: 13/30
(See Del. 131G)
W. 28c

214

ROYER-COLLARD

Cast bronze; height 12.7 cm
Markings: MLG; inside: 13/25
(See Del. 131L)
W. 29b

215

SOULT

Cast bronze; height 14.9 cm
Markings: MLG; inside: 13/25
(See Del. 131E)
W. 36c

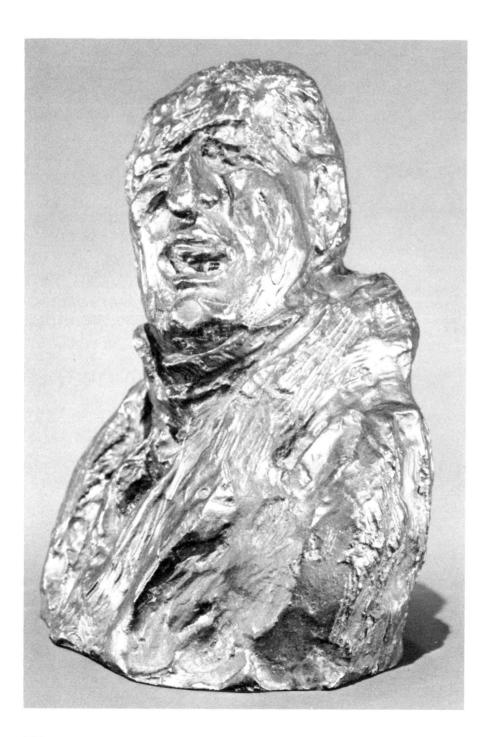

PODENAS

Cast bronze; height 20.3 cm
Markings: MLG; inside: 13/25
W. 27c

DELESSERT

Cast bronze; height 17.5 cm
Markings: MLG; inside: 13/25
W. 6b

218

FULCHIRON (TARTUFFE)

Cast bronze; height 16.2 cm
Markings: MLG; inside: 13/30
W. 13c

219

KÉRATRY

Cast bronze; height 12.2 cm
Markings: MLG; inside: 13/25
W. 19c

220

GANNERON

Cast bronze; height 17.9 cm
Markings: MLG; inside: 13/25
W. 15b

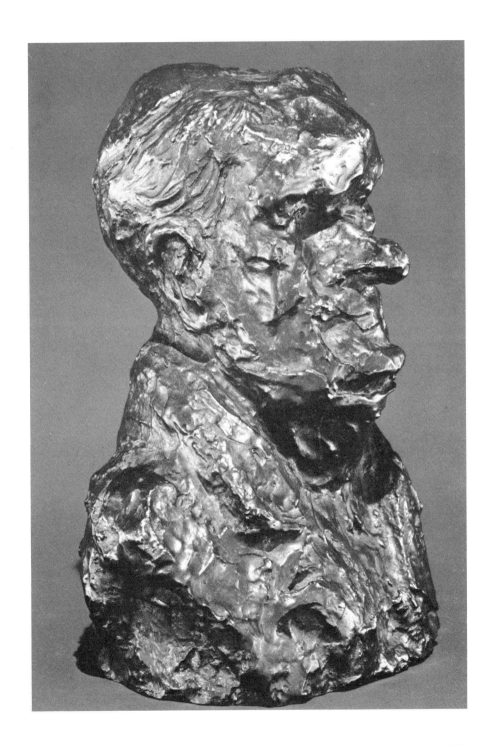

221

VIENNET

Cast bronze; height 20.0 cm
Markings: MLG; inside: 13/25
W. 32c

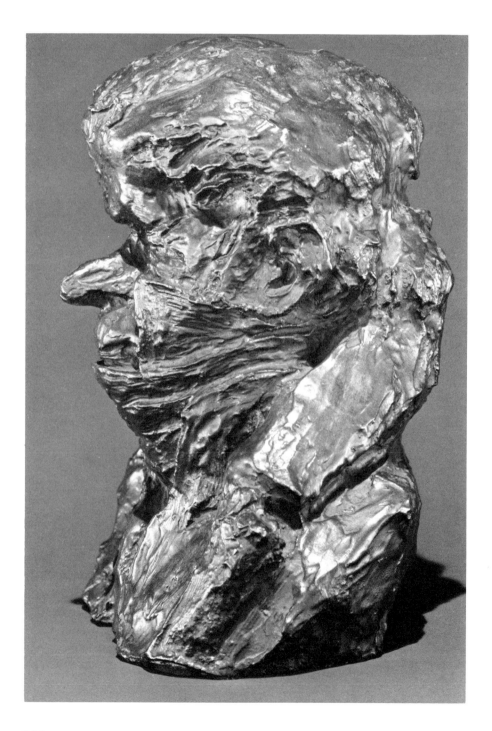

222

FRUCHARD

Cast bronze; height 12.7 cm
Markings: MLG; inside: 13/25
W. 12c

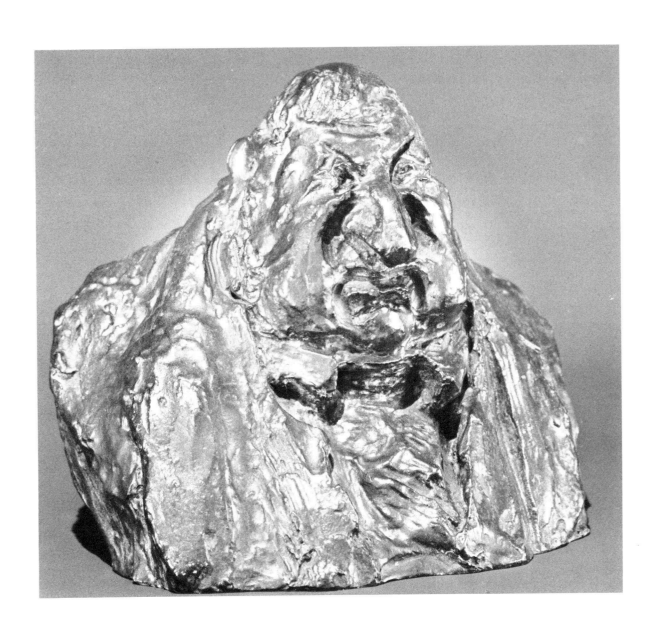

223

INCONNU "LE RIEUR ÉDENTÉ"
Unknown "Toothless Laughter"

Cast bronze; height 15.7 cm
Markings: MLG; inside: 13/25
W. 35c

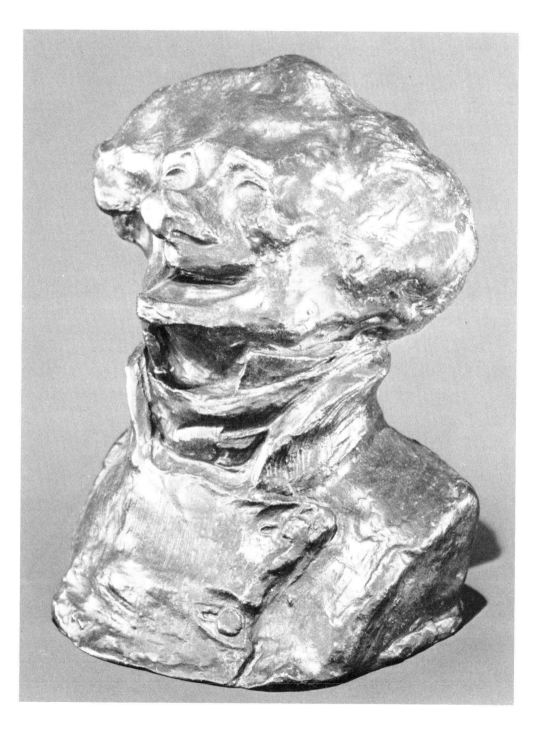

224

INCONNU "PELET DE LA LOZÈRE"
Unknown

Cast bronze; height 13.5 cm
Markings: MLG; inside: 13/25
W. 34c

CHEVANDIER DE VALDROME

Cast bronze; height 18.3 cm
Markings: MLG; inside: 13/25
W. 4c

PERSIL

Cast bronze; height 18.7 cm
Markings: MLG; inside: 13/25
W. 26c

LECOMTE

Cast bronze; height 16.7 cm
Markings: MLG; inside: 13/25
W. 21b

SÉBASTIANI
Cast bronze; height 12.8 cm
Markings: MLG; inside: 13/30
W. 30b

229

INCONNU "GIROD DE L'AIN"
Unknown

Cast bronze; height 12.7 cm
Markings: MLG; inside: 13/30
W. 33b

BAILLOT

Cast bronze; height 17.5 cm
Markings: MLG; inside: 13/25
W. 2b

FALLOUX

Cast bronze; height 22.7 cm
Markings: MLG; inside: 13/25
W. 11c

VATOUT

Cast bronze; height 19.4 cm
Markings: MLG; inside: 13/25
W. 31b

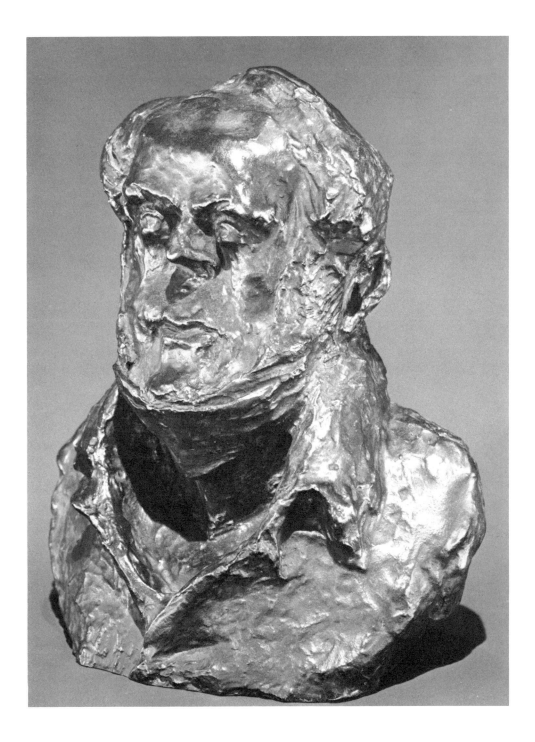

233

LEFEBVRE

Cast bronze; height 19.7 cm
Markings: MLG; inside: 13/25
W. 22c

234
MONTLOSIER
Cast bronze; height 19.0 cm
Markings: MLG; inside: 13/25
W. 23d

RATAPOIL

Cast bronze; height 43.5 cm
Markings: h. Daumier No. 0; right rear: Alexis Rudier
Fondeur, Paris
W. 37c

Note: First cast in bronze in 1891, this sculpture was modeled in clay in 1851 and cast in plaster shortly after.

LES ÉMIGRANTS
The Emigrants (second version)

Cast bronze; 33.0 x 72.0 cm
Markings: lower right: h. Daumier; lower left: Alexis Rudier
W. 39c

Bibliography

Adhémar, Jean. *Honoré Daumier*. Paris, Tisné, 1954.

_____ . *Daumier: Les Gens D'Affaires (Robert Macaire)*. Paris, Editions Vilo, 1968.

_____ . *Daumier: Financial and Businessmen (Robert Macaire)*. Paris-New York, Leon Amiel, 1974.

Alexandre, Arsène. *Honoré Daumier, L'Homme et L'Oeuvre*. Paris, Laurens, 1888.

Armingeat, Jacqueline. *Daumier: Moeurs Politiques*. Paris, Editions Vilo, 1972.

_____ . *Daumier: Les Gens Du Spectacle*. Paris, Editions Vilo, 1973.

_____ . *Daumier: Intellectuelle (Bas-Bleus) Et Femmes Socialistes*. Paris, Editions Vilo, 1974.

_____ . *Daumier: La Chasse Et La Pêche*. Paris, Editions Vilo, 1975.

_____ . *Daumier: Les Transports En Commun*. Paris, Editions Vilo, 1976.

Baker, C.H. Collins. *Lithographs by Honoré Daumier*. San Marino, Henry E. Huntington Library, 1948 (exhibition catalogue).

de Bainville, Theodore. *Mes Souvenirs, Honoré Daumier*. Paris, Chapentier, 1882.

Barr, Alfred H., Jr. *Corot-Daumier*, New York, Museum of Modern Art, 1930 (exhibition catalogue).

Baudelaire, Charles. *Curiosités Esthétiques*. Paris, Michel Lévy, 1868.

Bourgeois, Emile. *History of Modern France*, vol. I, Cambridge University, 1919.

Bouvy, E. *Daumier: L'Oeuvre gravé du maître*. Paris, Maurice Le Garrec, 1933.

Cain, Julien. *Daumier et Les Gens de Justice*. Monte Carlo, André Sauret.

_____ . *Daumier: Les Gens de Justice*. Paris, Editions Vilo, 1974.

Champfleury, J.F. *Histoire de la Caricature Moderne*. Paris, E. Dentu Éditeur, 1865.

_____ . *Catalogue de l'oeuvre lithographie et gravé de H. Daumier*. Paris, 1878.

_____ . *Catalogue de l'Exposition de Peintures et Dessins de H. Daumier*. Paris, Galeries Durand-Ruel, 1878.

Courthion, Pierre and Cailler, Pierre. *Daumier raconté par lui-même et par ses amis*. Paris, Cailler, 1945.

Claretie, Jules. *Peintres et Sculpteurs Contemporains*. Paris, Librairie des Bibliophiles, 1882.

Delteil, Loys. *Le Peintre-Graveur Illustré*. 11 volumes, Paris, 1925-1930.

Escholier, R. *Daumier, Peintre et Lithographe*. Paris, H. Floury, Editeur, 1923.

Feinblatt, Ebria. *Honoré Daumier: Exhibition of Prints, Drawings, Watercolors, Paintings and Sculpture*. Los Angeles, Los Angeles County Museum of Art, 1958 (exhibition catalogue).

Focillon, Henri. "Honoré Daumier." *Gazette des Beaux Arts*. Paris, 1929.

_____ . "Visionnaires—Balzac et Daumier." *Essays in Honor of Albert Feuillerat*. New Haven, Henri M. Peyre, Editor, 1943, pp. 159-209.

Fuchs, Eduard. *Der Maler Daumier*. New York, E. Wyhe, 1927.

Gobin, Maurice. *Daumier Sculpteur*. Geneva, Pierre Cailler, Editeur, 1952.

Hazard, N.A. and Delteil, L. *Catalogue Raisonné de l'oeuvre lithographié de H.D.* Paris, 1904.

Heiderich, Ursala and Schultze, Jürgen. *Die Lithographie von der Anfängen bis zur Gegenwart*. Bremen, Kunsthalle, 11 April-6 June 1976 (exhibition catalogue).

Ivins, William M. Jr., *Prints and Books*. "Daumier as a Lithographer," "Daumier—The Man of His Time," Cambridge, Harvard University Press, 1926, pp. 265-293.

Kaiser, Konrad. *Honoré Daumier Die Parliamentarier*. (Die Büsten der Deputierten der Julie-Monarchie). Berlin, Deutsche Academie der Kunst, 1952 (exhibition catalogue).

Klossowski, Erich. *Honoré Daumier*. Munich, R. Piper and Co. 1923.

Larkin, Oliver W. *Daumier Man of His Time*. New York, 1976.

Lejeune, Robert. *Honoré Daumier*. Lausanne, Éditions Clairefontaine, 1953.

Lemoisne, P.A. and Laran, Jean. *Daumier: Lithographies, Gravures sur Bois, Sculptures*. Paris, Bibliothèque Nationale, 1958.

Maison, K.E. *Honoré Daumier, Catalogue Raisonné of the Paintings, Watercolours and Drawings*. London, Thames and Hudson, 1968.

Roberts-Jones, Philippe. *Daumier: Moeurs Conjugales*. Paris, Editions Vilo, 1967 (exhibition catalogue).

Roger-Marx, C. *Daumier: Peintres, Aquarelles, Dessins*. Paris, Musée de l'Orangerie, 1934 (exhibition catalogue).

Roger-Marx, C. and Adhémar, J. *Honoré Daumier, Zeichnungen and Aquarelle*. Holbein-Verlag, 1954.

Roger-Marx, C., David Rosen and Henry Marceau. *Daumier*. Philadelphia, Pennsylvania Museum of Art, 1937 (exhibition catalogue).

Sadleir, Michael. *Daumier, the Man and the Artist.* London, Halton and Truscott Smith, Ltd., 1924.

Vallery-Radot, Jean and Roger-Marx, C. *Daumier, Le Peintre Graveur.* Paris, Bibliothèque Nationale, 1958.

Victoria and Albert Museum. *Daumier: Eye Witness of an Epoch.* London, 1976 (exhibition catalogue).

Vincent, Howard P. *Daumier and His World.* Evanston, Northwestern University Press, 1968.

Wasserman, Jeanne L. *Daumier Sculpture, A Critical and Comparative Study.* Greenwich, Connecticut, distributed by New York Graphic Society, 1969.

Wick, Peter A. *Honoré Daumier. Anniversary Exhibition.* Boston, Museum of Fine Arts, 1958 (exhibition catalogue).

Paper: Beckett Brilliant Opaque Vellum
Type: Andover
Printer: Southern California Graphics, Los Angeles
Designer: Warren Kennaugh
Publication Director: Sheri Hirst
Publication Assistant: Jane Seidel
Photographers: Seth Joel and Joel Breger